Other Lives, Other Realms

Other Lives, Other Realms

K A R E N   J O Y

MediaLuna

MediaLuna Pty Ltd
PO Box 756
Maleny, Queensland 4552
Australia

MediaLuna is a private press which only publishes commissioned works. It does not accept submissions of any kind.

First published by MediaLuna 2015. This edition published 2019

Edited by Ian Demack
Cover Design by NKDC. Creative Design & Strategy
Author photographs by Johanna H Studios (back cover) and Ian Demack (About the Author)
Typeset in Adobe Caslon Pro 12/17 by the publisher.

This work includes case studies. Names and identifying details have been altered to preserve the anonymity of those involved.

ISBN: 978-0-9942567-3-7

Dedicated to Ian

Contents

Foreword

I first met Karen Joy in 2009. I had just given a talk on dreams, and Karen arrived at the end just in time to hear the last few minutes. I think she was there to meet up with a friend and happened upon the talk, but that five minutes sparked a connection. I remember Karen looking through my books and asking some deeply probing questions, an eager and curious mind interested in science, research, and proof, on the one hand, and in trusting intuitive insight on the other.

A few months later, I was at a friend's book launch when I was introduced to her editor Ian. We got talking and Ian invited us to dinner to meet his wife. It was Karen. A welcoming feast was laid, and the conversations returned to the esoteric and Karen's search for proof.

At that time, Karen was the principal of a counselling practice, working full time in the practice as a psychologist and hypnotherapist, but in her heart of hearts she felt a calling to help her clients find healing through past life regression. She had accidentally taken a client into a past life during a regular hypnotherapy session, when she asked her to access the source of an issue in her life, and she observed the remarkable healing effect of this accidental journey.

Until then, Karen had kept her personal interest and experiences of past life regression separate from her counselling practice, but this accidental journey was a turning point, and a dilemma. Karen was faced with a choice. Which way would she go?

Karen was a popular columnist for Brisbane's *Courier Mail* for many years, writing about psychology and relationships, and she had written several books on relationships. Eventually it all fell into place: Karen would follow her heart, take further training in past life regression at The Newton Institute, do her own research with volunteers, and write up her results in a new series of books. The plan suited her nature to a T. Along the way, through her studies at The Newton Institute, she trained in Life Between Lives regression therapy, and that sealed her passion.

We've enjoyed many conversations about past lives and life between lives over the years, sometimes quite contentious, but always enriching.

So when Karen invited me to be one of the volunteers for her research, and to experience a Past Life Regression and a Life Between Lives Spiritual Regression under her guidance, I was excited and open-minded. I expected adventure and insight, although I had some doubts about whether I would be adventuring into past lives and life between lives, or whether I would be adventuring the magnificent realms of my unconscious mind as I roamed beyond the confines of my conscious mind. But then again, if you contemplate that for a moment, perhaps we're talking about the same thing, just using different words.

In the late 1990s, I was hypnotised six times into my future, an experiment I devised with an Erikson hypnotherapist as part of my research for my book exploring precognitive dreaming, *The*

Shape of Things to Come (Random House Australia, 1998). The results were interesting and challenging, and I knew I was a good subject for hypnosis, but I hadn't been hypnotised into my past, or into life between lives, and I wondered how different this might feel.

When I was hypnotised into my future, I was absolutely under, but I was in observer mode with no real sense of emotional engagement. Perhaps the hypnotherapist engineered the experience to create ideal circumstances for collecting the required data, but at the time, I thought this was the norm. So I was astounded by the profound emotion I felt when Karen first guided me into a past life.

The moment Karen landed me in a past life I could hardly speak for the emotional overwhelm I felt. Everything was intensely sensual, the colours, the air, the beautiful monastery garden, the monk's sandals I wore, the sense of being a man. I just cried, out loud, in Karen's chair, until I could find words to tell her where I was and what was happening.

Aside from the intensity, it all felt real, but at the same time I was conscious that I was sitting in Karen's room witnessing this experience. In many ways it felt like a lucid dream (having dual consciousness), but whereas a lucid dream feels both completely real yet you know it's a dream, this experience went even further. It felt like revisiting something that had actually happened, a life I had actually lived.

Was it a past life, or was it an intensely conscious dream experience, my unconscious mind reporting in the language of my dreams? It certainly gave me deep transformative insight into my life situation at the time. It was a journey into my spiritual nature, my soul life beyond my physical life. That is what matters, as I'm sure you'll agree as you read *Other Lives, Other Realms*.

Jane Teresa Anderson
Author of *The Dream Handbook*
JaneTeresa.com

Introduction

The only journey is the one within.

RAINER MARIA RILKE

Do you know that another world is waiting for you? A world where you feel loved and accepted. A world that gives you insight into the challenges you have faced in your life. Here your current life can be viewed through the prism of the many lives you have lived. In this world, wise entities guide and comfort you. Your life's purpose becomes clear. You feel appreciated and encouraged, even as some of the choices you have made in your life are being questioned. This is the world where you meet again with loved ones who have passed. It is a place of healing, of forgiveness and redemption. In this world you gain a greater understanding of the nature of reality. It is a world where your intuition is valued and enhanced.

This world is waiting for you at the end of your life. But you don't have to die to visit this place. This world is available now. Through the miracles of hypnosis and regression, which I discuss in the following chapters, you can visit this world with confidence, knowing that you will return safely from your adventures.

In the past, people called this place heaven. We call it our life between lives, the place you go after you die. There you review your last incarnation and prepare for the next. You gather with related souls and plan your next life.

On the way to your life between lives, you visit at least one past life. Reliving your past lives gives you important information about the themes running through your recent lives, themes that are playing out in your current life. These themes are explored in more detail during your visit to the realm known as your life between lives.

When you undertake this journey, you will return unharmed. But will you be the same? Probably not. Most people who return from this journey are transformed in a positive way. Most lose their fear of death. Many return with a clear understanding of their life's purpose, and with the enthusiasm needed to reach out for their goals. Some feel reassured about their life choices. Some feel determined to make changes. Many feel unconditionally loved and more accepting of others. Most feel a greater peace within themselves, and more settled in their lives.

This book is about transformative journeys to other lives, and to the realms we access during our life between lives. The journeys of many clients are explored, in detail or in part, in the following chapters. These are real stories about real people. They are drawn from the many regressions that I have conducted over the last seven years. I am extremely grateful to all the courageous clients who have taken a journey into other lives and other realms with me. Of course, the names of all these people have been changed, as well as any distinguishing characteristics.

I have endeavoured to relate each case as accurately as possible. Any changes I have made have been in the interests of clarity, while retaining the essential truth of the experiences recounted in this book.

As you navigate through the stories of people who have visited their past lives and life between lives, I trust you will glean useful information and insights from their journeys, and personally sense your connection with your higher self, your guides and your loved ones who have passed.

I suggest you begin by reading the following two chapters: *Hypnosis Demystified* and *Regression: A Step Forward.* These chapters explain how we can travel to other lives and other realms.

The chapter *Not Cleopatra* shows that even mundane past lives can reveal profound truths to us.

In *Proof,* I explore some of the evidence for the existence of past lives.

The cases cited in the chapter *Do Our Past Lives Affect This Life?* demonstrate how patterns established in previous lives can play out in our current lives.

Understanding Relationships explains how our relationships can carry over from life to life.

Using illustrative case studies, *Emotional Echoes* explores the origins of anxiety, depression and anger.

The chapter on *Healing* outlines some of the information clients have received about physical and emotional illness.

In *Facing Death,* the case studies demonstrate how experiencing other realms can reduce or even eliminate our fear of dying.

My Life's Purpose explores cases where clients discovered, often to their surprise, what they are really meant to be doing during their time on this planet.

In *The BIG Picture,* I share information that clients have been given about the nature of our reality here on Planet Earth.

Body Selection answers a question that troubles many people: 'Why have I been given this particular body?' If you have ever wished you were stronger, or more attractive, or more intelligent, this chapter reveals some startling insights.

In *Meeting Loved Ones* I lift the veil, and share the experiences of clients who meet their loved ones in the realm between our lives.

Off Track shows how you can help reset your compass, if you feel you're not achieving the goals you set for this life.

Redemption reveals how visiting your life between lives can help release crippling feelings of guilt, shame and unworthiness.

In *Soulmates*, I discuss the concept of an eternal, romantic partner, and detail two compelling cases.

When my clients are about to set off on their journey to other lives and other realms, I suggest they remain as open as possible to new concepts and experiences. And now, as you journey into this book, I kindly make that recommendation to you.

So remain open—and enjoy your journey!

Hypnosis Demystified

You use hypnosis not as a cure but as a means of establishing a favorable climate in which to learn.

MILTON H. ERICKSON, MASTER HYPNOTHERAPIST

Hypnosis is a very natural state of consciousness. We all go in and out of hypnotic states each day.

Have you planned to stop in at the supermarket while driving home? Suddenly you find yourself pulling into your driveway, and you realise that you completely forgot to pick up something for dinner. In fact, the car just seemed to be driving itself. You were in a trance. You were deep in thought and not paying much conscious attention to driving. Your subconscious has internalised the ability to drive and you were, so to speak, on autopilot. You were not fully in the present.

Now if you encountered something unexpected, a car coming right at you, for example, you would have popped out of the trance immediately and reacted to that emergency.

A hypnotic trance induced by a hypnotherapist is not all that much different. The hypnotherapist gently instructs you to relax your body. As you relax more and more, you gradually stop worrying about what is happening around you. Your attention shifts to your inner world.

The hypnotherapist will give you suggestions that align with your intentions for the trance. If you want to re-experience a past life, she will give you suggestions that accord with that, such as

1

'You will emerge into a past life that helps you understand your path in your current life.' If she suggests something completely unexpected and not aligned with your belief system, you will pop out of the trance. This is like the emergency when driving on autopilot. If you are severely challenged, you will react instantly to protect yourself.

We all know we have a physical body and we know our body is vulnerable. To survive, we constantly need food, shelter and protection. Our body can be damaged. Our body can die. Because we are vulnerable, we are usually alert and focused. We spend much of our energy looking after our physical self. That is why our instinct for self-preservation kicks in if another car veers across at us while we are driving, and we immediately brake to avoid a collision.

To freely enter into a trance, we need to know that we are protected, both physically and emotionally, from any harm. We need to feel that we are in a place that is completely safe and secure. We also need to trust that the hypnotherapist is going to follow our instructions, guide us into a trance that helps us meet our stated intentions, and bring us safely back to normal waking reality.

When we feel safe and secure, we can stop worrying about our physical or emotional safety and shift our attention from the outside world to the inner worlds. To travel to past lives and other realms, we need to focus inwards.

Hypnotherapists trained by the Newton Institute create a safe environment for their clients. I use a comfortable chair, soft lights, an essential oils diffuser and a quiet room to create a sanctuary of security and serenity.

Nearly all my clients go easily into a trance state and experience a regression. A few struggle to relax and let go. Here are some of the reasons why.

Some people remain hyper-vigilant. They're always watching for the sleight of hand. Intrusive thoughts—'something isn't right' or 'where is this taking me?'—keep their attention focused on the conscious world. Or they might expect to find themselves immersed in a deeply visual dream state, not realising that only a few people experience such vivid images. Even when they allow themselves to relax, they can block the flow of information by doubting the veracity of their experience. They believe they're making it up—it's just their imagination running away with them.

I encourage my clients to stop worrying about the reality of the information and images that are surfacing, pointing out that the word 'imagination' is closely related to 'image'. In a regression, clients need to open themselves to sensing images or information. They do this by using their inner eyes and their inner senses. It doesn't matter whether what is happening during the actual regression is 'true' or not. The whole process works best when clients are trusting, with few preconceptions. After they emerge from the trance, they make sense of the experience, and decide whether it feels true to them at a personal level.

A few people worry that something disturbing might confront them. I suspect they are unaware of an obstruction present in their current lives. Subconsciously, they know they have negative emotions that need to be released. Before leading anyone into a trance, I reassure my clients that I will take care of them, no matter what happens during the session.

I deal with disturbing experiences sensitively, using supportive techniques that ensure the client feels safe. Over the years, I have guided many clients through challenging histories and difficult past lives. In fact, I have faced many of these issues myself. Helping clients release disturbing emotions is most satisfying.

Clients who experience a disturbing past life or other challenges report robust benefits. They are relieved to free themselves from the past. Releasing any troubling emotions associated with our history has a positive effect on our current lives. The more disturbing the unresolved emotion, the greater the freedom we feel. Clients say they undergo deep, positive shifts once their emotions have been released and their experiences have been integrated into their lives.

One of my clients had a negative previous experience of hypnosis. He struggled to let go of those memories and place his trust in me. As a young man, he had gone out with his mates one evening to watch a hypnotist perform on stage.

An easy-going chap, my client immediately stepped up when the hypnotist called for volunteers. Stage hypnotists test these volunteers to find the most compliant. As a young man, this client was a bit of a larrikin who would have a go at anything. His attitude was perfect for the stage hypnotist, which explains why he was chosen. My client said he enjoyed the experience while on-stage. This view changed dramatically when his mates told him he had made a fool of himself. They laughed at him and belittled him. His mates, rather than the stage hypnotist, were the ones who did the damage. He swore he would never allow himself to be hypnotised again.

He came to me because he wanted to experience a past life.

In the pre-briefing he mentioned the stage hypnotist but he had forgotten the promise he'd made with himself. I spent quite a while inducting him into a trance before he said he couldn't allow himself to relax enough. I worked with him to uncover the reason and we discovered the steadfast agreement he'd made with himself to never again be hypnotised.

Promises we make to ourselves can be difficult to shift. They're more powerful than vows we take in public. They are more powerful because they're private vows that we take to mask our shame. After we've made such promises they fade from our conscious memory—but they'll emerge again to protect us when needed. Although my client wanted to access his past lives, that negative experience with the stage hypnotist was blocking him.

Once I understood the situation, I helped him remove the block. Eventually, he fell into a relaxed state. There was little time left but he still received some helpful information that moved him forward in his life.

I have had two clients who were unable to fully regress. Even though one had trouble letting go in the beginning, she experienced a past life in her first session. She found this experience to be both helpful and reassuring. However, during the second regression a couple of weeks later, she could not relax sufficiently to go inwards. She kept wandering off and could not focus.

The other client was not able to access a past life at all. He kept seeing scattered images and could not receive anything coherent.

In both these cases I moved directly to address the issues that we had discussed in the pre-brief. Because I have twenty years' experience as a psychologist, I used counselling techniques to resolve their inner conflicts. Both were happy with the results they achieved. When I followed up some months later, each noted that their lives had changed for the better.

I concluded that these clients actually needed psychological counselling rather than regressions. They did not, however, feel comfortable with science-focused, clinical counselling. In fact, one admitted he'd had negative experiences with counsellors in the past. I believe they chose past life and life between lives regressions because they identified closely with a spiritual approach. In any case, it didn't really matter. They both said they got what they needed.

This is my only guarantee regarding these regressions: *You receive what you need.*

Hypnotherapists who have been endorsed by The Newton Institute (TNI) to do life between lives regressions are well trained. To begin studying with TNI, one must have hypnotherapy qualifications and a hundred hours of documented hypnotherapy experience. The program of study includes many hours of training and many hours more of hands-on assessment.

TNI-endorsed hypnotherapists project a sense of confidence and security to their clients. As well as having years of study and experience, they are bound by a strict Code of Ethics. They belong to a worldwide community of life between lives hypnotherapists who share information, thereby continuing to grow and develop excellence.

Practitioners who are confident in their hypnotherapy work and who have taken their own therapeutic journeys, inspire trust and self-assurance in their clients.

I believe in divine guidance and divine timing, so I know clients will be guided to the right practitioner for them. Those who follow their intuitive guidance on such matters are wise.

Most people achieve profound outcomes when they find a therapist they can trust.

Regression: A Step Forward

Allow yourself to see what you don't allow yourself to see.
MILTON H. ERICKSON, MASTER HYPNOTHERAPIST

Regression is a specific form of hypnosis. Sigmund Freud coined the term 'regression' when he observed clients spontaneously age-regressing to an infantile state. Since then, many therapists have deliberately used age regression to help their clients heal childhood traumas.

To 'regress' literally means to return to a previous, less developed state.

Therapeutic regression is a complex process. Using hypnosis, the therapist inducts the client into a trance state. The therapist then guides the client back to the source of the stated problem, enabling any repressed, traumatic memories to surface. Usually, these memories include images and impressions of the incident, as well as the emotions connected with the trauma. The therapist helps the client release the associated emotions. By exploring various novel viewpoints, the therapist then helps the client gain a more complete perspective of the traumatic episode. Finally, the therapist encourages the client to integrate this new perspective into his or her life. Integration involves learning lessons from the traumatic incident and acting on this new information.

Many hypnotherapists who use age regression techniques stumble upon past life regression. Like Brian Weiss and Michael

Newton,[1] two pioneers in the field of past life regression, I unwittingly regressed a client into a past life.

My client had been compulsively helping other people to the detriment of her own family. She couldn't say *no* to her daughter's school, to friends or any others who needed help. She is a very capable woman, so needy people naturally gravitated to her. I guided her into a trance, and suggested that she go to the source of the problem.

As she goes back in time, I watch her become agitated and fearful. I expect her to go back to an event in her childhood. To my surprise she describes a setting that correlates with life in a peasant village hundreds of years ago. The villagers have been warned that barbaric tribesmen are marauding in the district and heading towards them. My client is an elder in the village and encourages everyone to conceal themselves. She suggests they hide under straw in lofts in the barn.

Her prescience is to no avail. The barbarians discover their hiding places and kill them all. My client is distraught. She cries deeply for several minutes. She eventually calms down when I suggest that her actions surely made no difference. All of them would have been found and killed, no matter where she hid them.

Soon after this session, the client reported that her behavior had changed significantly. She was more relaxed and more able to say *no* to requests for assistance.

As a result of this unusual regression, I found myself drawn into the world of past lives. Like other hypnotherapists who have discovered past life regression this way, I was hooked. The therapeutic results were so fast and effective that I could not ignore

---

1 Brian Wiess is a psychiatrist and Michael Newton was a clinical psychologist.

them. I read many books about past life therapy and eventually trained in past life regression.

During my research, I came across the books and work of Dr. Michael Newton. Before he developed life between lives regression, Dr. Newton practised past life therapy. During a past life regression, a client started describing a place that turned out to be her life between lives. Being a clinical psychologist with a respect for scientific research, Dr. Newton began investigating this phenomenon and documenting his cases. Eventually he wrote two groundbreaking books, *Journey of Souls* and *Destiny of Souls*.

Michael Newton conducted over seven thousand regressions. At one time he had people waiting three years to see him. He eventually founded The Newton Institute and developed the protocols, programs and ethics needed to pass on his knowledge to others. I feel privileged to have been trained by The Newton Institute. As a current member, I'm listed on the Institute's website.

Michael Newton developed a process that allowed people to be safely guided to their life between lives. This process uses deep hypnotherapy and should only be conducted by qualified hypnotherapists.

As part of the process, we guide clients to a past life. They experience death in that past life and then move naturally into their life between lives. Discarding the body is the usual entry into the life between lives state, and Michael Newton recommends this route, even when the death is metaphoric. He also recommends conducting a past life regression before the life between lives regression. This gives us two past lives to work with, and is especially important if the client has never been regressed before.

Whether the client has experienced hypnosis or not, we have found this prior past life regression enriches the experience and instills confidence in the client. Understanding the process pays off during the life between lives regression.

To appreciate the richness and variety of the realms that one can visit in the life between lives, it may help if you visualise a palace. Its many rooms are filled with a variety of different people. When you arrive, you will meet your spiritual guide who has been assigned exclusively to you, and who watches over you at all times.

He or she will lead you through the palace, beginning at the *gateway*. You might then visit the *rest home*, where you will be emotionally restored after an exhausting life. You may be taken to the *library*, where you may access information about the different lives you have led. There are realms where you can review your life, meet with others to plan your next life, or select the body in which you will incarnate.

You will be given opportunities to meet with soul groups, relatives, friends and loved ones who have passed. You may ask for advice from wise beings such as your spiritual guide or the Council of Elders. The Council of Elders includes a number of wise non-physical beings, usually five to seven. Some clients report that they meet the same wise elders after each life. Others say the Council membership changes. The Council is interested in your spiritual path and makes suggestions to help you meet your goals.

The real power of past life and life between lives regressions is experiential. Experience is the great teacher. Lessons are learned first-hand, and new understandings and perspectives arise spontaneously. Profound transformations can take place.

A life between lives regression is much like a near-death experience but without the trauma. Near-death experiences have been well researched. Kenneth Ring, formerly Professor Emeritus of Psychology at the University of Connecticut and the author of five books on near-death experiences, identified five stages that are commonly reported: peace, body separation, entering darkness, seeing the light and entering the light. Other researchers include a tunnel experience, an intense feeling of unconditional love and acceptance, meeting beings of light, receiving a life review, and receiving knowledge about one's life and the nature of the universe. These experiences are often present in life between lives regressions.

Kenneth Ring also observed positive changes in the people who underwent a near-death experience, including an increased regard for life, more compassion for others, a greater sense of purpose and self-understanding, a desire to learn, elevated spirituality, and heightened levels of intuition.

Most of my clients who have visited their life between lives report sensations and encounters similar to those on Kenneth Ring's list. Nearly all the benefits of a near-death experience can be gained from life between lives regressions.

One difference is clear: at the end of a life between lives regression, there is no need to decide whether you will stay in the afterlife, or return to your present life. At the end of a life between lives regression, you safely return to your current life.

There is another, more subtle difference between a life between lives regression and a near-death experience. In a regression, there is no sense of complete separation from the body as there is in a near-death experience. However, because you are relaxing in a comfortable chair in a secure room, your focus can turn away from the material world. Even though you are in a trance, you can verbally report your participation in the events that unfold. It is like being immersed in a compelling movie while pausing now and then to report what is happening. Your body and your immediate environment are forgotten. Your focus is absorbed with the journey you are undertaking.

Hypnotic regression is a marvelous tool that creates an opportunity to visit other lives and other realms. When conducted by a skilled therapist, the regression is safe and informative. Here perhaps is the new frontier, navigated not by ships or rockets, but by hypnotic regression.

Not Cleopatra

I wish everyone could get rich and famous and have everything they ever dreamed of so they would know that's not the answer.

JIM CARREY, ACTOR

'Why do so many people think they were Cleopatra in a past life?'

I have heard many skeptics express this view, or something similar. In some cases, they might be right. Some people probably do believe they were someone famous in a past life. General George Patton, for example, was convinced that he had previously lived as Hannibal, the great Carthaginian military leader.

Interestingly, none of the clients I have regressed has been taken back to a famous past life. But none have felt short-changed as a result. The past lives they experienced during regression, although seemingly ordinary, included moments of high drama.

All my clients have gained something profound from their regressions. The past lives they recalled helped them make sense of their current dilemmas, and offered them guidance for the next phase of their lives. Their past lives were as valuable to them as anything Cleopatra or Hannibal may have experienced.

The following cases reveal how unique and unexpected a past life regression can be.

Pattie

During a past life regression, most people experience just one life. Usually, this life is rich with challenges and learning. Pattie was different. Her guides took her to three lives, one after the other. Each life was unique. Despite the differences between these lives, Pattie, aged 55, found that each one provided her with some powerful insights.

Generally, I guide my clients to transition into their past lives by going through a tunnel. Pattie had some difficulty entering the tunnel. She found she could only pass through the tunnel on her hands and knees. The reason for this became evident when she emerged from the tunnel. She had been given the body of a lion.

> *I am outside and it is dark. I see moonlight and stars. When I come out of the tunnel I wake up inside a lion. I am a mature male with a big mane.*
>
> *It is night and I am looking out, over the savannah, surveying my kingdom. I am protecting two lionesses and three cubs. They are sleeping. I feel a strong sense of peace and contentment. There is nothing to fear; no predators to threaten me. I am watching the sky and making sure all is well before I lie down to sleep. I am happy being a lion. I have a deep, inner serenity.*

Pattie moved on to another life, this time as an Irish girl called Eliza. Born in 1809, the poverty she endured eventually drove her to steal some food. At sixteen years of age she found herself imprisoned on a ship sailing to Australia.

> *I have no shoes and my feet are dirty. I am wearing a raggedy, grey skirt. I am with other women sitting down in the bottom of this boat. It is wet and dirty. We are all wet and dirty, re-*

ally dirty. We are all sad. It is terrible in this boat. Others are sick and I cannot help them.

We progress to another scene in this life as Eliza.

I am sitting in a corner on the floor of a jail. That is where they sent us. Now I am seventeen. I am going to be whipped. They are so cruel. I tried to get some help for another lady. She is so old. Still they won't help her. I can see she is going to die. I am not allowed to even talk to comfort her.

We move on to another scene when Eliza is twenty-three.

I have a little house with my husband. We haven't got much but I can see lots of little yellow wildflowers. My husband is tall and wears his hair in a ponytail. He is about thirty. We are now both free but he still carries the scars on his back from when he was a convict. He is kind to me and taught me how to write. We have some land, just enough to make some money and live. We have gardens and I can see lettuce. My husband is very clever and makes things with wood. We married just a few weeks ago.

I asked Eliza how she met her husband.

He saw me in the big house. It is the biggest house in the town in New South Wales. Someone important had it. I think he was the Governor because he would get all dressed up. He had lots of convicts working for him and I worked in the house. People were nice to him but they said things behind his back. He was a mean man.

Research shows that Eliza was right. Governor Darling arrived in 1825 and assigned hundreds of convicts to chain gangs. He was hard on the convicts and he made many enemies in the developing colony.

We then proceed to the end of Eliza's life at the age of thirty.

It is daytime and I am sick in bed. We have a daughter aged three. My husband is very worried. My chest is not good and it is hard to breathe. I am going to die. I know my husband will look after our little girl. I did have a boy but he died two days after birth.

I know I have been kind in my life and I am not fighting it. I am letting go. I know it is time. I feel peace and no more pain. I die calmly. My husband is strong but he will cry later when no one sees him. My little girl doesn't understand but she will be okay.

I am floating. My spirit is free. It is swirling like it is dancing. I feel wonderful just being free, flowing in the breeze. I am part of the energy. It's good. I am dancing wild and free.

Pattie elegantly transitions straight into another life, her life as Rosa, a gypsy.

There is a campfire and I am dancing around it. My skirt is whirling out. I don't have a partner and it doesn't matter. I am free and happy.

I live in a gypsy van and it is fun. We travel from place to place. Sometimes the men trick the town people and take their money. They do it through gambling. Gypsy men are very tricky but they are not thieves. The men of the town think gypsy girls are easy but we are not. We are good girls. I am fifteen but I look older. I live with my family and I have a brother who would kill anyone who tried to hurt me. We travel all over but now I think we are in Spain.

We move to another scene in Rosa's life. Now she is thirty-nine and it is 1901.

It is evening, twilight. I have my own crystal ball and I can see the future. Some say they can do this but they cannot. But I actually can see the future and people pay me to do that. I am single. I didn't want to marry. I like being free. We still travel. All gypsies are one family. There are silly old gypsy men who fight sometimes. We laugh at them. Everyone else has children and the children come to me. I teach them and have fun with them and then I can tell them, 'Go back to your mother.' I am never lonely. I like being Rosa.

Another scene. Now Rosa is in her early sixties.

I am outside doing the vegetables with the other women. We chat while we do our chores. Women have a better life than men. Men think they are the bosses but they are not really. We privately laugh at them as we let them walk around with their chests puffed up like peacocks.

There have been wars so we travel a lot now. Some people don't like us anymore. We stay away from the cities. I am growing old but I still dance. Gypsy women always dance. I am happy.

Now we proceed to a time when Rosa is in her seventies.

I am walking in a little village in the south of France. The inhabitants are doing their usual rounds of the village. I am going to sell preserves, fruit made into jam. I am going into the shop that buys these preserves from me. I work on a farm and I am still fit even though I am old. The farmer likes us because we pick his fruit for him. We come here every year. He doesn't pay us much but we don't need much. He is a nice man.

We come to the end of Rosa's life. She is in her late seventies.

I am really old now. I have left the van. The farmer and his wife are looking after me. I feel tired. I am enjoying the sunshine of the day and I see that the flowers are out. This is my last day. I am alone, but I don't feel alone. I have had a full and happy life. Time to go. My spirit is whirling and becoming part of the energy.

Pattie meets her guide, who helps her assess those three lives.

The lion surprised me. There was a lot of strength in that lion but also a lot of peace. The stronger I get the more peaceful I become. It is an inner strength that comes from knowing who you are.

There was a lot of sadness in Eliza's life. I am being told that all life has purpose. Everyone is here for some reason. Eliza helped other people. In fact, she did too much for others and didn't look after herself. Because she never put herself first, she suffered. Even though she was a good soul, she was very much out of balance.

Rosa was a free spirit with a spiritual side to her life. Rosa trusted herself. She was strong enough not to follow convention. She was always true to herself, and true to others.

She was wise because she was an old soul. She lived many lives before she was even born.

Three months after this regression, I asked Pattie how she had been affected by reliving these lives.

I keep recalling the serenity and the peace that surrounded me when I lived as a lion. That life confirmed the inner strength that serves me so well in my current life. I can easily get that sense again. It is a sense of life being safe and non-threatening. The lion lived in a time before man. He had no predators.

The sad life as Eliza reminds me of my previous marriage in my current life. I was like Eliza in that marriage. I did everything for others and I fell out of balance. I know the cost of putting myself behind everyone else. I hadn't learnt that fully until this life. We can have good intentions to help others but we need to look after ourselves as well.

Rosa had a wonderful life. She was a very emotionally independent woman who was extremely happy. She didn't conform. She was herself. She found the right balance, being a good soul who looked after herself.

It is funny but I used to say, when referring to my previous marriage, 'My gypsy soul had been squashed.'

Pattie summed up the changes she experienced.

This has been a strong confirmation for me that what I am doing in my current life is right. I am on track. At this stage in my life, I am the happiest I have ever been. Like Rosa I feel I have the freedom to express myself openly and honestly.

Jared

Jared came to see me because he sometimes felt like 'dropping out'. He said he had 'perfectionistic tendencies' and was a bit of a dreamer. Whenever he failed to live up to his own standards, he felt like leaving this life. He wondered if this problem had come from a past life.

In the regression, Jared was taken to two past lives. In neither did he live for long.

In the first life, Jared is a young girl living during a time of turmoil between the local people of Europe and the Romans. The local villagers are rebellious and resist Roman rule. The Romans want peace so they can administer and exploit the land.

This young girl is different to most. She doesn't care about the Romans. She doesn't mix with the other children and makes no effort to appease the villagers. Her one love is nature. She takes pleasure in roaming the woods and being at one with the trees, plants and animals.

Her parents are locals but her father works for the Romans.

As she grows, the villagers became more suspicious of her. They gossip about her and call her 'a strange one'. Jared recounts her experience in a scene when she is thirteen.

> *It is night and I feel worried. I am with my mother in the cottage. She wants to keep me safe but the people of village don't like me. My beliefs are different. I love nature and I spend time in the forest. I am not interested in the boys or what the others want to do. The villagers think I am a witch.*

Her father talks to the villagers and tries to explain that she is harmless. Her mother also does her best to protect her. But her parents' support doesn't help much in an age where difference is feared.

By the time she turns seventeen, the villagers are restless and angry at being dominated by the Romans. They take out their anger on anyone they feel is an outsider. The young girl is condemned as a witch, along with others who do not fit in. Her father is away and cannot save her. Her mother weeps, and pleads for her life. Nevertheless, the young girl is beheaded, along with the others, by an executioner with an axe.

Her soul leaves her body. She is quite content to leave this life at a young age. There was no plan for a longer life.

In the second life, Jared is an accountant in New Jersey at the beginning of the twentieth century. He is only aged in his thirties but describes himself as old, ugly and unhappy.

He does not have a strong personality and tends to feel like a victim of circumstances. He is also idealistic and a perfectionist. He lashes out viciously at the only female close to him, his sister.

> *She is a floosie, an escort. She uses her feminine energy to make money. I am angry with her. I yell at her and push her down in the street. She falls on the wet cobblestones. She doesn't want anything to do with me anymore.*
>
> *Now I am alone. I didn't approve of her but I miss her. I liked her femininity but I didn't like her using it that way.*

His sister might have been a woman who sold her body for money, but she was also a loving, accepting human being who knew how to have fun. He misses her more as time goes on.

The accountant cannot take this imperfect life and kills himself before he reaches forty.

Jared has experienced two lives with sad endings. However, he and his guide are satisfied with these lives. The young female outcast remained true to herself by exploring her pleasure and connection with nature. She was far from perfect, as defined by the society in which she lived, and yet she was completely self-accepting. She achieved the goals set for that life, despite the abrupt ending.

The accountant found himself bound up in self-loathing and self-judgment. He was far too idealistic. He idealised female sexuality and judged his sister harshly for what he saw as her loss of purity.

In this life, he learned that judgment and perfectionism lead to deep dissatisfaction and unhappiness. The clear message was to learn to be more accepting.

Keith

Keith came to see me during the Global Financial Crisis. His work had dropped off and he wondered if there were any past life issues blocking him from succeeding. He was in danger of losing heart and he didn't want to become negative about winning more work.

I regress him back through some neutral childhood memories to his time in his mother's womb.

He describes the womb as dark and comfortable. He cannot see much, but feels safe and warm. He is in the third trimester.

I ask him how he feels about being born into a physical body again.

I feel excited. There are things I can do in a physical body that

I can't do as a spirit. I know it is not as comfortable with a body but there are things I want to experience.

When I ask about his mother, he says she is worried about having a baby. He will be her firstborn. But she is also excited and looking forward to it. She worries about the birth and whether it will hurt and whether she can feed him and bathe him. She is missing her own mother who lives a long way away.

I also ask him about his purpose for this life as Keith.

My purpose is to experience. I am not a big planner. I like being spontaneous and letting life unfold.

We progress into a past life.

All is dark and the sun is just coming up. I am a man, alone, wearing brown boots. I am in the country. There are horses and a farm. Earning a living is difficult. It is the 1800s in the American west. I am waiting for something...rain. I am waiting for rain. I see dead trees and grey, hard ground. No crops. I am a settler, a lone settler. I have some flour, tea and sugar, and a well. I have some seed and some horses but not much more. I feel it will rain but it is going to be rough until it does.

Keith's name in this life is Jeremiah Smith. We proceed to a significant event in his life as Jeremiah.

I have come to town. I am wearing new clothes and I have money in the bank. All is going well. The rains came and I worked hard. I had three years of good crops. I am talking to the bank manager. He is very friendly but I am here for business. Someone has made a good offer on the farm and I am seriously thinking about selling it. I know the rains are unreliable.

We move onto the next significant scene in Jeremiah's life.

I am back east, somewhere in Connecticut. I have bought an apple orchard that has a cider press. I am married. The woman I married was a widow and she has two healthy sons. The boys are good hard workers and very helpful in the orchard. We all work the property together. The weather is more reliable here. I am not passionate about my wife but she is a good woman. I decided to marry her because I knew she would look after me. I am not as thin as I was out west. She cares about me and cooks good food. We get along well with each other. I am happy.

We move to the last day of Jeremiah's life.

I am ill. I know I am going to die. I am not good at saying fancy things but I tell my wife and the boys that they have been good to me. I was very lonely before they came into my life. They figure out that I love them even though I don't actually say it. I am okay to go. My life was hard when I was a kid but it has turned out well. I have had a happy life.

Jeremiah passes over gently into his soul state. Keith is directly informed about Jeremiah's life and the lessons learned.

Jeremiah had it tough when he was a kid. He had to trust himself. It was hard being alone. With a partner and the boys it got easier. He could have walked off the farm out west but he trusted it would rain and it did. He got out while it was good. He waited until the right time to get out. He didn't panic.

Jeremiah learnt patience. He trusted his judgment and he had wisdom. He achieved everything he set out to do. His only regret is that he didn't get closer to people.

I remind Keith that he wants help in his current life. I ask what he needs to know in this regard.

I have this vision of a green field like a meadow. It is lush, a place of opportunity and safety. I am being told that there are opportunities to be realised. I need to offer what I have to the world and see who accepts my offers. I know what to do. I need to be patient and trusting.

Keith got exactly what he needed. The story of Jeremiah was extremely reassuring. Keith experienced a lot of powerful feelings during the session that taught him more than he could have learned at a purely intellectual level. He received a very clear message to remain confident within himself, and to trust that opportunities would arise.

Two months later, Keith reported that he had a lot more work and he was confident that even more would come.

Keith's life as Jeremiah was not complicated, although it had its challenges. He was an ordinary man living an ordinary life, and yet the experience of this simple life proved profoundly reassuring to Keith.

Conclusion

Pattie, Jared and Keith all left my office feeling positive about their regressions. They all gained something precious from reliving their seemingly ordinary past lives.

One can understand Pattie being happy with her experience. The lives she revisited were not highly dramatic. Even her life as the lion was relatively uneventful. Nevertheless, each life provided her with important information. She knew she was on track with her current life. There is perhaps nothing more satisfying than carrying within you a sense of being exactly where you need to be, and doing exactly what you need to be doing. Pattie received the reassurance she was seeking, and treated it like gold. Would she have gained anything more from discovering that she had lived as Cleopatra in a past life? Of course not. The three lives she experienced reaffirmed her sense of self-belief.

Jared was content with his past lives, too. His first, as a young woman who never fitted in, gave him the confidence and courage he needed to be himself. In the second, he committed suicide. Still, this experience encouraged him to value life and not take it for granted. It also showed him that he needed to be more flexible, and less focused on perfection.

Keith also got what he needed from his past life. He was reassured that the rains will come, the work will find him and his skills will be valued. He felt positive and reassured and remained so until the work arrived as promised.

Each client received the support they needed to take the next step in their lives. They didn't need to know they were someone famous in a past life. A past life regression is not a frivolous matter. Our journey into a past life is sacred. We are opening up our spiritual connections and our spirit guides respond appropriately. They give us what we really need.

As we progress through life, many of us reach a point when we want to know more about who we are, and what has shaped us. When we regress back to a past life and to our life between lives, we are given a deep understanding of the themes playing out in our different lives, and the goals we have set in our current life. This knowledge allows us to move on with our lives with renewed energy and purpose.

It is possible that Pattie, Jared and Keith have experienced a life as someone famous or heroic. Perhaps you have too. Even if you have, it will probably remain unexplored if you undertake a regression unless it is specifically and currently relevant.

So far, no one I have regressed has needed to revisit a past life as a famous person. All my clients received exactly what they needed from their ordinary past lives.

Proof

Everything we call real is made of things that cannot be regarded as real.

Niels Bohr, Quantum Physicist

Is it possible to find proof for the existence of past lives, or for lives of healing and reconciliation that take place between our incarnations?

These days, information about reincarnation and life after death is readily available. Many books have been written about past lives. A few have been written about our life between lives. Anecdotal stories of children who remember past lives can be viewed on YouTube. The late Dr. Ian Stevenson of the University of Virginia spent forty years researching reincarnation. He documented over two thousand cases of children who provided credible evidence of their past lives. Nevertheless, such ideas are considered unorthodox, and many people remain skeptical.

Very few mainstream educational institutions are interested in researching non-physical reality, reincarnation, and life between lives. People who conduct such research rarely belong to academia. Some have little or no academic background. Many have left mainstream science.

Collectively, researchers such as Michael Newton, Robert Monroe, Brian Weiss, Bruce Lipton, Rupert Sheldrake and Thomas Campbell have made a great contribution to the understanding of non-physical phenomena. If you are looking for evidence of the non-physical, I can recommend their work.

Not everyone needs scientific evidence to convince them that other dimensions exist beyond our conception of physical reality. Some people are in tune with their deeper selves. They know that we are more than just our physical bodies.

In the past, I was fairly skeptical. Over the years, however, I have encountered a great deal of anecdotal and scientific evidence of paranormal phenomena. This opened my mind to the possibility of non-physical reality. Then I gathered my own personal evidence through paranormal experiences, self-hypnosis, lucid dreaming and regression. Even so, I value evidence over blind faith. I think it is important to keep the door open to new information and possibilities. I like to remain in a state of learning.

Ultimately, we need to reach our own conclusions about the existence of life before and beyond death. Information gathered during regressions can provide convincing evidence for other lives and life between lives. Here are a few examples.

Bella

Bella experienced a past life as a nurse in the Second World War. After I guide her into a trance, she finds herself with a group of displaced people near the end of the war. They are hiding in a forest because they are afraid of being caught by their enemies. They walk for miles behind the tree-line, too frightened to venture out into the open, where they might find something to eat. Because Bella is a nurse, others in the group look to her for leadership. But she does not know whether to rest or to keep moving, or which way will lead them to safety. She decides to forge on, hoping to find some food. It makes no difference. Eventually they all weaken, and die of starvation.

When Bella comes out of the trance she comments on the uniform she was wearing in that life.

'It was very distinctive. There was an apron-type thing with a cross on it. And a cap. I would know it if I saw it.'

I suggest we look on the Internet for pictures of nurses from the Second World War. We find pages and pages of images. I point out different possibilities that seem to match her description. She rejects them all until finally she sees a picture of nurses from Scotland.

'That's it!' Bella exclaims.

Bella is shocked. The nurses wear a shirt with a Peter Pan collar, an apron with a cross on the bib and a basin-style cap. This is the uniform she saw.

The picture is from www.maybole.org. The nurses are photographed in front of the Turnberry Hotel in Scotland, which was used as a hospital during the war. We could not determine whether any of these nurses were in Europe after D-Day.

Karen

Personal experience can be a powerful convincer, as I discovered some years ago during my first visit to my life between lives. When the practitioner took me back to my immediate past life, I was surprised to find myself living as a male during the Second World War. Even more astonishing, he served as a German infantry soldier on the Eastern Front during the invasion of Russia. During the invasion, he witnessed a scene that shocked him.

I am standing looking at a group of captured Russians. Apart from their Captain and one of the men, they are all sitting on the ground facing me. Their hands are on their heads. The Captain is kneeling on the ground, attending to some injury on the back of one of his men. The Captain has his back to me. Beside me, on my right, is a German soldier with a rifle. I feel no fear.

The captain's uniform is very strange. He wears a blue cap and a jacket that is off-white with a bluish tinge. I can't believe that anyone would choose such a pale colour for a uniform. War is a grubby business. A light colour like off-white is so impractical. It doesn't make sense. I must be making it up.

Now I am feeling uneasy. The German soldier is pointing his rifle at the Captain. He is going to shoot him. I want to stop him, yell out and say 'No!' It doesn't seem right to me, shooting a man in the back, a man that is our prisoner, our responsibility. Before I get anything out, he shoots the Captain in the back. That must have been a signal because now I hear machine gun fire. I am aware of two German soldiers, one on my far right and one on my left. Each is aiming a machine gun at the Russian prisoners. They are mowing them down, killing them all. I don't feel a part of this slaughter even though I am a German like those murdering these men. I am shocked. Dismayed. It is wrong.

After the regression, I undertake some research. I find out that Russian prisoners were often shot by the Germans. I also learn that Hitler gave a specific order in 1941 that all Commissars were to be shot. The Commissars were officials of the Soviet Communist Party.

I have a strong sense that I fought at the Battle of Stalingrad in my previous life, and died there in December 1942. The German invasion started in June 1941, so I work out that this incident must have happened in the 18 months between June 1941 and December 1942. I search the Internet until I find a picture of a NKVD Commissar Captain. The NKVD was a Soviet law enforcement agency, closely aligned with the secret police, and part of Stalin's apparatus of political repression. It was later renamed as the KGB. The uniform I discover exactly matches the one I saw during my regression.

The Commissar can be seen in the picture on the previous page. His jacket is a bluish-tinged off-white, and his cap and trousers are dark blue. This uniform was only in use in 1941 and 1942. The picture is from a painting by the talented Russian artist, Andrei Karashchuk (used with permission).

I feel shaken. Up until this point, I was still not sure if past lives really existed. Perhaps we make it up, I'd thought. I know I have never seen this picture before in my current life. With this hard evidence, something shifts inside me. I cannot deny it anymore. I surrender to the idea that I have lived before.

David[1]

David experienced a past life as a Catholic monk called Desmonte.

It is 1560 and Desmonte is travelling around the Bohemian countryside visiting Catholic churches. He is secretly gathering

---

1 You will meet David again in several future chapters.

information about the excesses of the priests. He notices that they wear elaborate robes and their churches are ornate. He also sees that the peasants are poor, hardworking and suffering economic hardship. He believes the priests are exploiting the piety of the masses.

He returns to Prague in 1564 to make his report. He sees a large crowd gathered around people in stockades. There is social upheaval and he cannot find the religious people with whom he is aligned. They have been replaced and now are in hiding or have fled. There are two factions in the church, one given to power, the other devoted to spirituality. Desmonte belongs to the latter faction, hoping that the church will experience spiritual renewal. Unfortunately for Desmonte, his faction is losing ground.

Desmonte never finds his allies. Eventually, he leaves Prague, and dies many years later in Spain.

When David returns to do a life between lives regression, he tells me he has been researching his past life as Desmonte.

It all makes sense now. It was the time of the Counter-Reformation in the Catholic Church. But during the regression, I kept doubting the information I was getting. It seemed a bit strange being a devoted, spiritual monk who was spying on others in the church.

The Counter-Reformation was an attempt by the Catholic Church to regain its power in the face of the Protestant Reformation. It ran from 1545 to 1563, and while a number of administrative reforms did take place, they did not herald the changes that Desmonte and his colleagues hoped for.

David is one of those people who easily receives names, dates and details during regressions. Not everyone has this capability. David spent many lifetimes in monasteries. I wonder if his ability to observe and record detail was developed in those quiet, secluded lives.

Terry

Terry had lived previously in the thirteenth century[2]. During his regression, Terry found himself embarking on a journey to Jerusalem with many others. Together they rode into battle, and brutally conquered a mighty city. When Terry emerged from the regression, I asked him what he knew about the crusades. He said he knew nothing about them. Returning home, he began to research their history.

In the course of his reading, Terry came across some old illustrations of Istanbul, previously known as Constantinople. He immediately recognised it as the place where he had fought as a crusader. The crusaders were merciless. Terry admits that it was so disturbing that he didn't want to see what he had sensed during the regression.

> *I fought against the information I was receiving. I thought I must be making it up. But I remember the city vividly. It had a cathedral with a great copper dome. When I did some research I realised that the city was Constantinople, not Jerusalem. The cathedral was the Hagia Sophia.*

The Hagia Sofia dates back to AD 537. Terry was a part of the Fourth Crusade that sacked Constantinople in 1204. The Fourth Crusade originally intended to conquer Muslim-controlled Jeru-

---

2 This life is explained in more detail in the chapter, *Emotional Echoes.*

salem. Instead, the crusaders were diverted to Constantinople. A historian described this infamous event:

> *They rushed in a howling mob down the streets and through the houses, snatching up everything that glittered and destroying whatever they could not carry, pausing only to murder or to rape, or to break open the wine-cellars...[3]*

Even though Terry knew nothing about the crusades, I sensed that the experiences he was reporting during his regression related to a life as a crusader. However, he didn't mention the word 'crusade' at any time during the regression and neither did I. In fact, the crusaders never used this term. They described themselves as Knights of Christ and saw themselves as undertaking an armed pilgrimage. The Christian military campaigns against Islam during the Middle Ages were not described as 'crusades' until 1638—four hundred years after the Fourth Crusade!

After undertaking his research, Terry was convinced that he had not made it up. The doubts he experienced during his regression proved to him that he had relived a genuine past life.

Ashleigh

Ashleigh experienced a life as a woman during the American War of Independence.

The scene opens when she is in her early twenties. She is watching a battle that is taking place in a field. She is not afraid, just curious. She notices, with some surprise, that on one side the soldiers are dressed in uniforms with red jackets. The others are <u>not in uniform</u> and look less professional.

3 Steven Runciman, *A History of the Crusades, Vol. 3*, Cambridge University Press, 1951, p 123.

I ask her whose side she is on. She doesn't know. I prompt for more information. She struggles to make up her mind. She says she doesn't really care who wins. Ashleigh is young and never studied English or American history.

After the past life, Ashleigh and I discuss her experience. She says she found it difficult to accept what she was getting. She thought she was making it up. It was true that she was struggling to receive the information. I had to intervene frequently to help her maneuver around her blocks.

Even during the regression, she thought it was very strange that she didn't know which side she supported during the battle between the redcoats and the militiamen.

I recall the case of Andrew[4], one of my other clients, who had regressed to a past life during the early days of the American War of Independence. I describe his experience to Ashleigh.

Andrew is on the side of the rebels and against the redcoats. He says many settlers have not yet decided who to support. The redcoats are advancing, and Andrew is riding back to his farm. In the distance, he sees a small contingent of redcoats ride up to his neighbour's farm. He feels he should intervene but knows he cannot. He has an essential role to play in this war. Andrew knows his neighbour tried to sit on the fence because he was afraid to take sides.

Andrew lies low and watches. His neighbour's indecision does not save him. The redcoats drag him outside and execute him.

Ashleigh is reassured by this story. She can see that her indecision actually makes sense. She was living at a time when

---

4 Andrew's past life is explored in more detail in *Redemption*.

the settlers were loath to take sides. They didn't understand all the issues and they were afraid to commit to one side, as they had no idea who would prevail.

When Ashleigh came back to do her life between lives regression, her skepticism had been resolved. The regression proceeded smoothly without the blocks and confusion that accompanied the past life regression.

Proving that we retain consciousness during the period between incarnations is more difficult than validating past life experiences. Individuals can find evidence, however, in the form of predictions that are subsequently found to be correct. An example is my own life between lives regression, mentioned earlier. I felt overwhelmed by my responsibility for my elderly mother. She was suffering from dementia, and had few financial resources. During my regression, the Council told me that my mother would be well cared for, and subsequent events proved this to be true.

Conclusion

Many people experience doubts while they are in the trance. They worry that aspects of their story are not making sense. Such doubts block their progress and need to be put aside. They are always surprised and reassured when eventually the story does make sense or when their subsequent research bears out what they saw in the session.

I can also be surprised. I have had my initial doubts about a past life later overturned.

As noted earlier, in my previous life I served as a German soldier in both the world wars. During the regression my therapist asked me what I did between the wars. 'I am a soldier,' I replied.

I have studied both world wars in some detail and I had some doubts in my mind. I had assumed that the Treaty of Versailles prohibited Germany from having a standing army.

I was wrong. When I looked it up, I discovered that Germany was allowed to have a standing army of one hundred thousand men after being defeated in the First World War.

I also learn that soldiers were trained in Dresden. This explains another mystery for me: Some years before I knew about these past lives, I experienced a compelling sense of déjà vu when I first visited Dresden. I knew I'd been there before.

Clients have told me that they have visited cities for the first time during their travels, only to discover that they immediately felt right at home. They knew exactly where to go and what scenes would unfold as they walked around a corner. The city fitted them like a glove. Such experiences can act as evidence of past lives.

People who visit their past lives and life between lives often begin to trust that they will endure after their current physical lives come to an end. Those who doubt are often opened up to greater possibilities. The more they open their minds, the greater their chance of having more affirming experiences.

We all need to do our own research and come to our own conclusions about the nature of our universe. While scientific evidence can be helpful, nothing quite beats the experience of remembering a past life, which reveals personal historical truths we had not previously known.

Do Our Past Lives Affect This Life?

Everything that is today could not be if it were not for that which was before.

ABRAHAM, CHANNELED BY ESTHER HICKS

From guiding many people through regressions, I have seen how our experiences in one life can influence our following lives. Quantum physics has revealed the amazing underlying reality of our world. Research by scientists such as Dr. Bruce Lipton and Dr. Ian Stevenson shows us how our past lives can affect our current lives.

Scientists tell us that everything is made up of energy. Quantum physics reveals that our material world is not really solid. Atoms, the basic component of the universe, are 99.99% space. Like an empty room containing air, an empty atom still contains something, namely an electromagnetic field. I think of this field as vibrational energy that we just perceive as solid and substantial.

Our emotions and thoughts also have a vibrational frequency. This we know intuitively. Our knowledge is reflected in our use of phrases such as 'we were on the same frequency' or 'I sensed a strange vibe when I walked into the room'.

Dr. Bruce Lipton, biologist and researcher into stem cells, is the author of *Biology of Belief.* In that book he explains how our identity, our 'self', is not physical. He means we are more than our physical bodies. A membrane containing many receptors covers our cells. These receptors pick up vibrational signals from the environment. This environment includes our thoughts and emotions, which are vibrations. The membrane-covered cells are analogous to a TV set that picks up signals from a transmitter. What is this transmitter? Our true self. Our true self is not contained in the body. We could also refer to our true self as the soul. Dr. Lipton writes:

> *My self exists in the environment whether my body is here or not. Just as in the TV analogy, if my body dies and in the future a new individual (biological 'television set') is born who has the same exact set of identity receptors, that new individual will be downloading 'me'. I will once again be present in the world. When my physical body dies, the broadcast is still present. My identity is a complex signature contained within the vast information that collectively comprises the environment.*[1]

Our thoughts, emotions and experiences combine to create an informational package of vibrational energy. It is part of our soul's fingerprint.

In his book, Dr. Lipton suggests that evidence for the 'broadcast' of an individual continuing even after death can be found in the experience of people who have had organ transplants.

The Heart's Code, by Paul Pearsall, supports the idea that our individual personalities find expression at a cellular level. Pearsall shares stories about people who received organs transplanted from deceased donors. There are many examples of people who begin to exhibit aspects of the personalities of their organ donors.

1 Bruce Lipton, Ph.D., *The Biology of Belief*, Mountain of Love/Elite Books, 2005, p 191.

Dr. Lipton draws a powerful conclusion: 'Cells and organ transplants offer a model not only for immortality but also for reincarnation.'

When we complete each life, the quality of our soul is changed by that Earth experience.

Dr. Thomas Campbell, the physicist and out-of-body researcher, theorises that the purpose of incarnating multiple times is to refine the quality of our consciousness, thereby lowering the entropy of the universe. Wisdom is the sole catalyst for refining our consciousness. Our wisdom increases as we gain knowledge and experience, and as we reflect upon all we have learned. Our consciousness is a culmination of all our previous experience.

Our memories of patterns of behavior, emphatic decisions, emotional stances and trauma are vibrations that manifest in the cells of our bodies, right from birth. The late Dr. Ian Stevenson, researcher into reincarnation, suggested that memories, habits, and even birthmarks can be carried over from past lives.

It appears that memories carry over when they have not been fully addressed and previously resolved. Resolution comes when we have the time, strength and inclination to explore and integrate the issue into every aspect of our being. If we turn our attention away from the issue, it remains repressed. This affects the quality of our soul. To be free, we need to resolve our issues at some point—maybe in our next life, maybe in a thousand years. To the soul, time is immaterial.

'Very well,' you might think, 'but what about these lives we have between our lives? Can we resolve these issues after we die and before our next incarnation?'

Even if it is possible for souls to work on resolving issues in between incarnations, they need an Earth experience to test their progress. Our lives on this planet are intensely physical. This physicality enables us to separate good intentions from true resolve.

When we plan our lives at the soul level, we set up situations that will force us to confront our unresolved issues. For example, imagine that a young woman died of starvation in a past life. A fear of not having enough food might carry over into her next life. Initially, this fear lies dormant. Then one day, while still quite young, she hears her mother cry out because the cupboard is bare. Although this only happens once, this incident awakens her latent fear. As an adult, she begins hoarding food, without knowing why. Hoarding is her strategy for dealing with the underlying fear.

However, her fear still needs to be resolved. When her hoarding becomes a problem, this prompts her to address her fear of starvation. She might seek help to understand her behavior. What kind of help? A regression is one way of revealing the source of her hoarding behavior and resolving her fear.

Intense emotions, if they are not resolved, can easily be carried over from one life to another.

One of the most dangerous things you can do in life is to make a curse. Curses have great power because of the intense emotion that accompanies them. A curse can reverberate through subsequent lifetimes. Once the individual is aware of the curse and sincerely revokes it, the curse will no longer be active.

As the following case shows, the greatest effect of the curse is on the person making it.

Jaya

Jaya visited a past life where she suffered so deeply that she ended up railing against God.

Jaya lived as a pioneering woman somewhere in North America a couple of hundred years ago. The scene opens with Jaya burying her husband, who has died from a sudden illness. Apart from two children, a boy and a girl aged nine and eleven, she is alone. They live in an isolated cabin built on a gentle knoll that rises above the alluvial plains. A river curves around the perimeter of the property.

On a fine sunny day, the children are playing down by the river while Jaya is working in the vegetable garden near the cabin. Suddenly, Jaya sees a wall of water explode down the river. After the regression, she describes it as 'like a tsunami'. She rushes down to the river, now flooded, calling for her children. They are gone. No matter how long she searches, they are never to be found.

Jaya is totally bereft. She has lost her husband and now her children. Her shock turns to anger. She cannot accept her loss. She is furious with God's unfairness. She stands outside, near the river, looking up at the sky. As she shakes her fist at God she curses Him, vowing to never love children again. She is done with life and dies soon after.

In the next life, Jaya is a man. Tall, slim and sinewy, he lives alone. Cut off from his family and with no friends, he finds work wherever he can as he wanders from place to place. Living in various boarding houses, he keeps to himself.

This man feels very little for other people. He is empty and numb. There is only one thing that arouses his emotions—something too terrible to contemplate.

A soft, kind smile from a child hits him like lightning. He feels a quick softening inside him that he cannot tolerate. There is only one way to deal with this feeling. He kidnaps and kills the child. It is all about reclaiming his power. He feels driven to kill the feeling of love that briefly rises up in him and he does this by killing what he perceives as its source—the child.

One day, a child with a warm, loving smile comes up to him and gives him a flower. He feels himself soften for a moment. This feeling is terrifying. A deep yawning gap opens up in him. It is the emotion of loss, the great loss he suffered in the previous life. Of course, he doesn't realise this. He just feels the deep pain. He is compelled to kill this feeling in himself. He captures a beautiful young girl of about eight or nine. He takes her away and, to his surprise, she remains open and trusting. She doesn't seem to have any fear. Even as he kills her, there is a gentle questioning in her eyes. He is completely shaken. Shattered, he finally realises what he has been doing. The guilt he feels is heavy. His career as a child killer is over.

Soon after, the authorities accuse him of murder and he is tried and is hanged.

He refuses to leave his body. He is terrified of hell, as he is sure that is where he is headed. Jaya is physically shaking with fear as she is recounts his demise and death. Eventually, after being sufficiently reassured, he floats away.

Jaya learns that she was carrying some of the guilt and fear passed down from this man, who had not been able to release it. For some time, she had been carrying an enormous fear of getting into serious trouble. She irrationally felt she might be sent to jail, or die. These emotions needed to be released. During the session, she feels an immediate sense of relief. Now, to be fully resolved and whole, she needs to come to terms with the criminal behavior of this man and find within herself the compassion needed to accept and forgive him.

Other emotions and attitudes can also be carried over between lives. In the following case, the major recurring emotion is guilt associated with the use of food.

Lionel[2]

Lionel is overweight. He seeks a past life regression to gain a deeper understanding of his relationship with food. He intuitively feels that his weight problems originated in a past life.

In an earlier incarnation, Lionel lives as a nobleman in France around the fourteenth century. The scene opens on the evening of his sixteenth birthday. His father has put on a lavish display and invited all the important people to the celebration. A few people seem genuine and they greet him warmly. He soon realises, however, that nearly all of the guests are there to gorge themselves on the banquet and play politics with their associates and rivals. He is annoyed that his birthday is the excuse for their antics, and disappointed that his father is a part of it all.

This is when I start to become contemptuous. Some of them think they are so clever they can dance words around you. It is not worth responding. As soon as you do, you are part of their game. They think they are cleverer than those who don't play.

2 You will meet Lionel again in the chapter, *Healing*.

They like to insult the ones who are genuine. They think I am stupid and not aware of what they are doing. I want to get away but I am not supposed to leave. I am a showpiece. That annoys me. Luckily they are not coming near me.

The tables groan under the weight of all the game, fruit and cheeses displayed on silver platters. Most of it will be discarded after the party. This upsets Lionel further. His father has over-catered deliberately: he wants his guests to notice how wealthy he is. Being excessive is part of the game. Lionel feels revolted. He is well aware that the ordinary people have very little.

They treat food like a weapon. They consistently give too much to themselves and too little to others. Then take it away from others as if it was just a game. They don't care about the effect on others. If they see the effect, they justify it. They think they are better than everyone else. They think they are entitled to more. Power and entitlement go together. It is a game to them.

The scene changes. Some years later, Lionel is in charge of some of his older brother's estates. He refuses to play the political games so beloved by his noble contemporaries. He cares about the people on his lands and doesn't want to exploit them the way that others would, were they in his position.

I don't want to play their little games. I want to make things run smoothly out here. I want this place to be home for people.

Unfortunately, Lionel and his people pay a high price for his fine principles. His lands are ravaged. Spanish soldiers on their way to fight a war up north pass through his estate, looting the farms and villages.

I feel like this shouldn't have happened. I feel it is my fault but I don't know how I could've stopped it. All the people are now gone. Their houses are empty. Everything was taken. They have nothing. Their food is gone. Everything is gone. There is no reason for them to come back. I should have stopped it.

Lionel is sure that the looting of his lands was less an act of thoughtless plunder than an act of treachery. One of the French nobility, who has a Spanish wife, encouraged the soldiers to come through and ravage the lands. Lionel was forewarned but could do nothing about it. He had no powerful allies to help defend his people. He has no friends to help him now seek justice. He knows he will get nowhere if he confronts the powerful people who allowed the soldiers to pillage with impunity. They will just deny any part in it.

Lionel is very disillusioned. He has never liked the way the world is. He cares about the poor people. He had tried to change one little part of it where he had some authority. But his good intentions came to nothing.

Years go by and Lionel's older brother dies. Now the lands could pass to Lionel. But to take possession of the lands, he will need to play political games. He will need to form alliances against his cousins, who are maneuvering to seize the lands for themselves. He has to make up his mind to either plot and scheme to win what is rightfully his, or to walk away. He fears that if he stays he will need to compromise his values. If he leaves he will leave the fate of his people to others who do not care for them.

The next scene occurs after many more years have passed. Lionel is old and coming to the end of his life. He is not ill, but knows he will die soon. He lives in the castle because he won the title to his lands. He decided to stay and played the necessary political games.

Every day since then I have paid a price. Playing the game has become my life. Now I am one of the ones I feel contempt for. To be fair to my people I must often be less fair than I would like.

Lionel thought he was helping his people, but because of the decisions he has been forced to make, some of his people now hate him. He withheld food from his people to gain their compliance. He held lavish banquets, just like his father did, to shore up his alliances with the powerful nobility.

If you don't have extravagant banquets, the nobility discounts you. And you need them for trade and defence. I don't know how I am going to die but I am so tired, I cannot keep going on. I don't have it in me.

When he finally dies in his canopied bed he is greatly relieved to pass over.

As he draws parallels between his past and current lives, Lionel realises that he uses food as a weapon. In his past life he used the threat of starvation to punish his people. He hosted sumptuous banquets to win favours from his fellow nobles. He hated himself for this. In his current life, he punishes himself by overeating.

I am bringing all the guilt I felt in that life into my current life. When I use food as a weapon in this life, I feel the same as

*I did in that past life where I used food as a weapon. The more
I use food as a weapon, the worse I feel about myself.*

In his life between lives, Lionel is told his dysfunctional relationship with food has arisen in several lives. He has developed
a tendency to see food as a symbol rather than as the sustenance
it really is, and this is playing out in his current life. For him
food can symbolise punishment, a solution to a problem, or a
much-desired reward.

In the next case, we are given a glimpse of all the human incarnations of a soul. This illustrates how recurring patterns of behavior
develop over a number of lifetimes.

David

David had visited two past lives and his life between lives. You
might recall David from a previous chapter where he was the
monk, Desmonte, in one of his past lives. In his life between
lives, he is given vivid information about all his previous past
lives. This broad view paints a clear picture of his spiritual development over a series of lifetimes.

In his first incarnation, David is a Roman centurion wearing
a bronze helmet, crested with flamboyant red plumes. He has
great courage, fighting in many battles. With his men, he is often
victorious. He remains in warrior roles in subsequent lives and
continues to develop his courage.

After many lives as a warrior, he finds himself in a slightly
different role: a spy. Again, he has several lifetimes spying for one
side or another. He is caught and dies in many of the early lives.

Gradually, he develops his spycraft. He learns to read people accurately, and this skill is carried over into subsequent lifetimes.

As a spy, he betrays others and is betrayed. He decides he needs to atone for the sense of guilt that gnaws away at his soul. He starts incarnating in religious roles, often as a monk. Over several lifetimes he lives as a devotee of all the major religions: Christianity, Judaism, Buddhism, Hinduism and Islam. He meets many inspiring people and comes to believe that he can free himself from the physical realm. He becomes a seeker of enlightenment.

Now his bid for enlightenment guides him through several lifetimes. During these lives, he gradually becomes more solitary and reclusive. He learns that this pattern of seeking solitude is also carried over from life to life. As he learns to love the monastic routine, he loses touch with the courage he developed in his early lives as a warrior and spy.

In his second-last life before his current life, he feels deeply let down. His many lives as a monk have left him increasingly disillusioned with the religious path. It is the time of the Reformation. He is exposed to the politics and hypocrisy of those in the church. He has an opportunity to develop new directions, but he falls back on his old patterns. Some time after his sessions, David reflects on what he has learned.

The lifetimes revealed to me by my guide showed an incremental progression, with many of my habits, strengths and weaknesses crossing lifetimes. Many of my career choices were similar across lifetimes, starting from the military, progressing to intelligence gathering, and to religious institutions. I only shifted my life purpose when my circumstances during the Reformation provoked an epiphany. However, I still struggled to break the habits I'd developed during my previous lives.

David was fortunate enough to be given an overview of all his lives during his sessions. He could clearly see the connection between each life and the patterns he developed.

The regressions of these three clients give us a glimpse of the powerful effect our past lives can have on our current life. A few other cases, briefly reviewed below, confirm this power. They help demonstrate that numerous challenges, including emotions, memories and patterns of behavior, can be carried over from lifetime to lifetime.

One client had many lifetimes as an alcoholic. In his previous life, he had died penniless and drunk. Even his knowledge of this repetitive, destructive pattern of behavior was not enough to permanently break this long-standing habit.

Another client came to see me because he had lost his purpose in life. A regression revealed that he was here to help his brother, Jack. Jack didn't cope well with setbacks in his physical lives. When things became too tough, Jack took an early exit. There were several lifetimes where he demonstrated this pattern of bailing out, including the First World War when he climbed out of the trenches to run into enemy fire. My client had lost his way after Jack committed suicide a few years earlier. Wearily, my client informed me, he would be coming back in his next life to try once more to help Jack stay grounded.

Two of my clients experienced past lives where they were pregnant. Both were nearly full term when they died. The first starved to death at the end of the Second World War. The second was of high birth living in Ancient Egypt. Her noble origins could not save her from a fatal illness. At the moment of death, neither wanted to leave her body or her baby. Such grief, carried over from moments of trauma, manifested differently in their current lives.

The first developed an eating disorder when she and her husband decided to try for a baby. She spent more than a year intermittently overeating until she came to see me. I took her back to her death from starvation in the Second World War, which gave her the opportunity to release her grief over her lost baby. She later told me that she conceived on the evening after our session. She gave birth to a healthy baby girl, and her eating disorder never returned.

The second became emotional whenever she was near a baby. This tearfulness had occurred all her life. She felt embarrassed because she didn't understand her tears. Once her past life grief was released, the sadness she'd felt around babies vanished completely.

Conclusion

Many people have benefited from discovering and releasing issues that had their genesis in past lives. Brian Weiss, author of *Many Lives, Many Masters*, and Michael Newton, author of *Journey of Souls*, have publicised this powerful phenomenon. Every day, practitioners trained by the Newton Institute confirm the benefits of exploring our past lives. Once they are liberated from their blocks, fears and emotional reactivity, people can approach their lives with a renewed sense of purpose. From my personal experience of accessing and releasing my own past life traumas, I can attest that the benefits are real and permanent. Every time I released a past life issue, I felt lighter, more confident, and filled with a sense of freedom.

I have noticed that some clients sense intuitively that certain issues manifesting in their lives are related to a past life. They may have tried more conventional psychotherapies, without isolating the cause of their distress. I always trust a client's intuition and, almost without fail, their intuition is correct.

However, many clients encounter and release past life issues that were not evident before they came for their session. Only after they emerge from their trance can they see the relationship between their past lives and their current life. They are always pleased to be relieved of these unanticipated and unresolved issues.

It is worth remembering that positive patterns of behavior also develop over many lifetimes. David, for example, learnt to cultivate courage during his many lifetimes as a warrior. Although the effect was dissipated during his religious lives, he was soon able to reconnect with that courageous energy and make the significant changes needed to get his life back on track. His case also demonstrates how we develop skills that carry over from life to life. He developed the ability to maintain order and routine. From his monastic lives, he also learned to be independent and enjoy his own company, with no fear of loneliness. Of course, making progress requires us to find the right balance between competing demands, and now David now needs to develop his relationship skills.

I can only be in awe of the creation of this amazing universe where we are given unlimited opportunities to develop and evolve. Eventually we can enjoy this wonderful physical reality by learning how to create the experiences we desire, without the traumas we suffered in past lives.

Understanding Relationships

There is only one happiness in this life, to love and be loved.

GEORGE SAND, NOVELIST

One of the most difficult challenges we face in our physical lives is navigating our relationships with others. Accessing our past lives and life between lives can shed light on our current relationships by providing us with information about our behavior over many lifetimes.

As we go through life, we develop different strategies for interacting with other people. Some of these strategies serve us well; others may be destructive. Without realising it, we may act out these negative strategies in our intimate relationships. If we keep repeating these strategies, they become a habit, or pattern. Once we become aware of these negative patterns we want to change them. But change can be difficult when the origins of these patterns lie deeply buried in our soul memory.

A regression can illuminate our personal history, and give us a better understanding of our most challenging relationships.

The following case studies show how the insights gained during a session can help us address problems in our current relationships. In addition, some of these case studies show how reliving the past can help us release unwanted, negative emotions.

Lola

Lola realised that she was attracted to needy, pushy people. She came to her session hoping to understand the genesis of this pattern, and why it kept playing out in her life, with predictable results.

In her relationships, she would do everything she could to keep her partners happy. It never worked. No matter how much she gave it wasn't enough, and her relationships always ended badly. Lola was keen to change this dysfunctional dynamic.

While Lola was in the trance, I asked that she be given the answers she needed. She was guided to the house she lived in when she was seven years old.

Lola is in the lounge room, dancing around in front of her parents and brothers. She's the fairy princess. As she pirouettes she senses the energy of her aunt, who can be a nasty, pushy woman. The aunt had recently visited the family and had managed, as usual, to greatly upset Lola's mother. Lola's mother and the aunt are sisters. The aunt has always been extremely jealous of Lola's mother, believing her to be more attractive and more popular.

While Lola is dancing, she senses a dark presence behind her. She dares not turn around. Instead, she focuses on the sunlight pouring through the doors and windows. She wants to stay facing the light because it brings her happiness.

I check to make sure that she feels safe and strong. Lola nods. Then, I encourage her to turn around to face that dark energy. She wants her question answered and the answer is there but she has to be brave enough to see it.

She senses a monster behind her. When questioned, she describes it as ghostly and wispy grey, with gnashing teeth.

Eventually she summons up the courage to turn around and face that monster.

When she shifts her attention, Lola sees two older females in the hallway behind her. The hallway is a dark tunnel, and the two women are filled with a sullen desperation. Lola describes them as grinding their teeth and clawing at the walls. Their arms are spread out in wild disarray. Lola stands rooted to the floor, staring, as they advance slowly towards her. She senses the terror that underpins their longing.

She becomes aware that these two women are her grandmothers. They are begging for her forgiveness.

Her paternal grandmother is easy to forgive.

This grandmother died before Lola was born. Lola's father loved his mother and always spoke kindly of her. The grandmother seems to pick up Lola's feelings of compassion because she gradually changes colour, from grey through blue, mauve, pink to peach. She slowly fades away and Lola senses that she is now at peace.

Her maternal grandmother is in much more turmoil. She would find it difficult to accept forgiveness, even if it was offered. Although Lola would like to forgive her grandmother, she does not feel forgiving. She has some compelling reasons for her reluctance.

Lola has always sensed a coldness in her mother and her maternal grandmother. She never felt loved by her mother, and she knows her mother never felt love from this grandmother. Lola needs to understand why they were both so emotionally distant.

Suddenly, Lola finds herself in her maternal grandmother's house. She sees her grandmother as a younger woman, desperately scrubbing clothes on an old scrubbing board. Lola intuitively knows her mother was a child at this time.

Her grandmother's hands are red and raw. She is washing the clothes of her husband and eight children. She has to get it all done. She is a devout Christian and she must make sure everyone is dressed in clean, neat clothes so they can go to church.

Her entire focus is on pleasing her husband. The Bible says this is her duty. The family goes to mass every morning before they go to school or work. They are all perfectly groomed so others will admire them, and her husband will feel proud of his family.

Every evening they all sit down at the dining table. Lola's grandmother has prepared the dinner, making sure everything is perfect. After dinner the males sit around and talk while the females clear and wash up. The work for Lola's grandmother is never ending.

Lola sees that her grandmother is emotionally shut down. Her grandmother feels safe focusing on external appearances. She never stops to notice her feelings or those of her children. Her whole identity is caught up in pleasing her husband and impressing the other churchgoers.

Lola's mother and the other children, including the nasty aunt, grow up feeling unloved. They all shut down emotionally to varying degrees.

Now that Lola understands, she feels compassion for her grandmother. She opens her arms and hugs her closely, offering deep love and forgiveness. The grandmother sobs. Lola feels her grandmother's pain and cries too, until all their grief is released.

Lola now sees images from her current life. Everything falls into place. She realises that she spent her childhood turning away from any negativity. Instead, she focused on being as happy and as light as possible. Being positive was her survival strategy. She needed to feel safe, even though she lived with a mother who was clearly disturbed and unable to give her the love she needed.

Lola carried this strategy into adulthood. As a child, she turned a blind eye to her mother's faults. As an adult, she overlooked the faults of her partners. As a child, she took full responsibility for making her mother happy. Later in life, she believed she had to make her partners happy.

As a result, Lola remained in relationships with pushy and needy people, long after an emotionally healthy person would have left. But pushy and needy people felt familiar to Lola. Her relationships always ended badly because the people she chose as partners were always fundamentally unhappy.

The compulsive desire to keep one's husband or partner happy was an emotional need that had been passed down her maternal line. At this point in her life, Lola had a young daughter. She was pleased to know she was not going to pass this problem onto her daughter.

Now that Lola understood the genesis of her behavior, she was determined to change. She soon left her abusive partner and started valuing herself. She put healthy boundaries in place so any future partner would treat her and her daughter respectfully.

Stanley

Stanley's wife encouraged him to undertake a life between lives regression. She'd found her session beneficial, so Stanley decided to give it a go, despite his skepticism.

During the regression, his guide took him back in time to a poignant experience in his current life. He found himself at his mother's deathbed. He said he remembered seeing hatred in her eyes.

After making this statement, Stanley went silent. I sensed he was receiving some important information. Eventually he spoke.

I am being told that what I saw in her eyes that day was not hate. She saw me coming into the room and she wanted to sit up to greet me. The look in her eyes was pain. She felt a lot of pain while making the effort to sit up. She wanted me to have a good memory of her. She was trying to look after me. She loved me.

I saw what I wanted to see. I felt a lot of guilt. I hadn't visited her much. I was busy and travelled a lot. Even when she was dying, I didn't stay long. I thought she was angry at me for not spending time with her. But it wasn't her. It was all me.

Stanley had tears running down his cheeks. He was relieved his mother loved him and that he no longer had to carry his heavy burden of guilt. He said he was now at peace.

Stanley was genuinely surprised that the regression enabled him to let go of this sad episode in his life. During regressions, many people are given the opportunity to release emotion from old, unresolved wounds, whether they were inflicted in their current life or in a past life.

Adrianne

Adrianne wanted to undertake a past life regression because she was caught in an emotional triangle with two other women. Tall and confident, Adrianne worked as a social worker, so caring for others came easily to her. She explained how normally she was positive and happy, but this emotional dilemma was bringing her down.

Adrianne was deeply committed to her female partner, Erin. Erin had her own successful business and travelled frequently. Adrianne and Erin had been together for a decade and were now married.

Two years ago, a new employee, Cassandra, started working in Adrianne's workplace. Adrianne felt immediately drawn to Cassandra and they quickly became good friends.

Although she was very competent in her job, Cassandra was sometimes nervous and very talkative. Adrianne didn't mind. When Erin was travelling interstate, Adrianne was delighted to have Cassandra's company to go to the theatre, the shops or to chat over coffee.

Right from the beginning, Adrianne felt connected to Cassandra at a soul level. She felt so comfortable with Cassandra, and talked so much about Cassandra, that Erin eventually became concerned about the nature of the relationship.

Adrianne insisted she was not attracted to Cassandra in any sexual way. She only wanted a close, platonic friendship. But it was evident to both Adrianne and Erin that Cassandra harboured a strong sexual attraction to Adrianne.

In their daily life, Erin was making a lot of noise about Adrianne's relationship with Cassandra, not understanding why she just didn't give Cassandra up. The arguments were starting to affect their marriage. Adrianne wanted to please her life partner but felt an overwhelming sense of grief at the thought of not seeing Cassandra again.

Eventually, she agreed to give up her friendship with Cassandra but it didn't last. Adrianne received a birthday card from Cassandra. Gradually Adrianne and Cassandra started phoning and texting. Adrianne wanted to see Cassandra again but before meeting her, she decided she should be honest with Erin.

Erin was devastated. She told Adrianne she loved her enough to let her go to be with Cassandra if that is what she really wanted. Adrianne never wanted to lose her marriage to Erin but she didn't want to lose Cassandra either. She was caught again, right in the middle, feeling that she was being pulled apart.

Adrianne sensed that the drama she was playing out with Cassandra was karmic. She hoped a past life regression would throw some light on the situation.

The regression took Adrianne back to her life as Beth, a young woman who lived in an English town in the 1890s.

I am living with my husband and younger sister in the poorest part of town. The dwellings are small and cold and butted up against each other. The building seems to be set near a cliff and there are many steep steps in the back yard.

Many children in the town are ill. Some die. I am scared for my sister. She is young and frail. She is like a daughter to me. I don't want her to become ill. I am so anxious, I am frantically cleaning the house. I am also obsessively looking after my sister's wellbeing. I am preparing special food for her. I am

64

making sure she is dressed warmly. I am not allowing her to go out into the cold and rain. I will do anything to prevent her getting ill.

In spite of all Beth's efforts, her sister soon begins to ail.

She has developed a fever. Now she is coughing. I am sick with worry. I am doing everything I can to help her. I am coaxing her to drink water and giving her food that she doesn't want to eat. Now I am sitting beside her. She is in bed and she looks so weak and pale. I pray she won't be taken, but I can see she is slipping away.

Adrianne cries.

She is dead. There is nothing I can do. I can't believe it. I am so sad. She was so young. She didn't deserve to die. I miss her so much. My husband is trying to help me but I find no solace in his efforts. I am always crying.

The years pass and I am still crying. I just cannot get over the loss of my dear sister. My husband cannot understand. I am inconsolable.

Beth died at age forty. She was glad to go. It was a life of so much sadness.

I see my sister. The first thing she says is 'It's not your fault.' Everything is all beautiful and white. Now I see my husband passing over and he is sorry for not understanding.

Beth drifts towards the light. Her guide appears, and explains the purpose of Beth's life.

There was a plan. Beth's life was about grief, learning to deal with grief. The death of her young sister was the obstacle that Beth was supposed to overcome. She failed. She never got over the loss of her sister.

The guide is telling me that the grief has to be resolved. I am here with you now, sitting in this chair, experiencing all this so I can resolve it.

Beth's sister is the same soul as Cassandra, and Beth's husband is the same soul as Erin.

The guide is telling me that there is something I need to do. If I want to progress in my current life, I have to do this. It will resolve what was unfinished in Beth's life. I need to let Cassandra go.

Adrianne cries deeply for several minutes. Grief is not easy for her. She'd told me earlier how deeply upset she had been when her grandparents died some years ago. Suddenly she feels her grandparents near her.

They are hugging me and telling me how much they love me. I feel so much love from them. It seems like they are really here.

I silently give Adrianne time to cry. I know she is feeling the intense feelings of joy, light and love that come from above.

As her grief subsides, Adrianne says she can now understand why Cassandra's arrival into her life had created so much turmoil. She now knows for sure that she and Cassandra are soul-related. And she knows that she will see Cassandra again at the end of her life.

Adrianne is also clear that she is meant to be with Erin. In this current life, they are a married couple again. They have an opportunity to experience the love and intimacy they had missed out on in Beth's life.

Adrianne felt peaceful but drained when she came out of the trance. She knew exactly what she was going to do.

Erin will not be home until later. I have an opportunity and I am going to take it. I will visit Cassandra on my way home, hug her and say goodbye. The karma from Beth's life is finished.

Adrianne's intuition was correct. There were important soul relationships in play in her current life as well as unresolved issues from a past life. Once Adrianne had freed herself from the past life grief and understood her purpose this life, she was easily able to implement the changes needed to get her life back on track.

Sherenne

Sherenne, aged forty-one, sought a past life regression to gain more clarity about her current life. She specifically wanted to understand her relationship with Cliff, a fifty-four-year-old divorcé with whom she was living. Although Sherenne loved Cliff, at times he could be nasty and abusive. He was easily offended, and responded viciously when triggered. His previous wife had been unfaithful and had cheated him out of money, so he was not very trusting.

Sherenne regresses easily to her past life as a woman aged twenty, named Mara. Her bare feet are covered with a dark blue robe. This robe completely covers her from head to toe with just a slit near her eyes so she can see. She is alone inside a house with open windows. Looking out a window, she sees nothing but sand and desert. She notes that the climate is very hot and dry. She can see other houses and feels she belongs to some sort of community. The houses are made out of an earthy material and all look the same.

Although she lives in this house and feels at home, Mara knows it is not her house. She takes care of it and the man who lives there. He is Ahmad, aged forty. Although they have a sexual relationship, they are not married.

Mara does everything she can for Ahmad because she owes him.

From the age of three through to sixteen she lived with relatives who disrespected and mistreated her. Mara is light-skinned while her relatives are darker. They make it clear that they deeply dislike her and her light-skinned mother. She doesn't know why her mother left when she was three, and has been waiting many years for her to return.

Ahmad is a business associate of her relatives. He visited their home many times over the years and saw the way Mara was treated. Although Ahmad is a hard man, he didn't like the way the males in the household looked at Mara as she grew older.

When she is sixteen, he tells her the truth that her relatives have been keeping from her. Her mother is dead. She died when Mara was three. Mara grieves deeply for her dead mother. Ahmad offers to buy her off her relatives and take her with him. She cannot forgive her relatives for playing with her emotions so cruelly, and willingly leaves.

Mara's life is better with Ahmad. She has more freedom and can walk to the market to buy food. She gradually grows to love him.

We move to a time when she is in her mid-thirties. Ahmad is sick and she is taking care of him. He cannot do anything anymore. Although he is mean sometimes, she puts up with that because she feels she owes him a debt for rescuing her. He dies. Time passes.

> *I am in the same house and on my own. People don't have anything to do with me but I don't mind. I have everything I need. I can read. He taught me to read. He taught me everything and I am grateful. I am always by myself but people are beginning to get a certain amount of respect for me. Although they don't have anything to do with me, they no longer walk away.*

We move to the end of Sherenne's life as this desert woman, Mara.

> *I am very old, in my nineties. I missed him a lot. I didn't like living so long. I am not diseased or sick, just old and tired.*

She passes in her sleep. As she becomes her eternal soul-self, Sherenne realises that Ahmad in that desert life is the same soul as Cliff in her current life. She also sees that her mother in her current life shares the same soul as the mean adoptive mother in the desert life. Her mother in her current life is not a happy person.

With the help of her guide, Sherenne assesses the past life and looks at parallels with her current life.

She notes that as a child in that past life as Mara, she endured some terrible experiences in the hands of her relatives.

When Ahmad offered to help her, she seized the moment. This is an important lesson for her current life.

> *I have taken an opportunity for a better life in being with Cliff. I am supposed to look at my life in a more positive way.*
>
> *Cliff tries to help but I don't see it as help. I don't feel that I owe him, and because of that I don't allow myself to open to what he offers. Just because he is a hard man doesn't mean he doesn't care. He is hard because he thinks he needs to be. He is only protecting himself.*
>
> *I don't need to feel I am less than anyone else. I have a vast potential within me that is still untapped. I need to trust, open up and let my abilities unfold.*
>
> *I need to learn that I will be let down at times. There will always be disappointments as this is a part of life. It is not personal. There are ups and downs. If I close myself off so that nothing bad ever happens to me, I shall never get to experience life as I am meant to. I am being told I will always get through.*
>
> *My guide is saying that I need to say positive things to myself everyday. I can be envious and jealous and I need to work on that. I need to say good things about myself out loud. I have no need for envy and jealousy and I will overcome them if I do what my guide suggests. I have a lot of inner strength.*

From her session, Sherenne realises that she can persevere with the relationship with Cliff. They both are closed to some degree, as they were in their past life together. In that life, Mara felt inferior to Ahmad, and some of those feelings of inferiority have carried over into Sherenne's current life. She has few financial resources while Cliff is a very wealthy man. The power imbalance that prevailed during her past life is playing out again in her current life.

After Ahmad died, Mara spent many years alone, and built a lot of independence. This tells Sherenne that she could walk away from Cliff if the worst came to the worst, even though she would struggle financially. But walking away from Cliff could mean remaining closed. Being in a relationship forces her to open up.

The same is true for Cliff, who pulls away to protect himself. By staying with him and deciding to be more accepting and open, Sherenne can give Cliff an opportunity to gradually rebuild his trust. The relationship presents a chance for each of them to progress along their spiritual path by learning to be tolerant, generous, and accepting of each other.

Conclusion

Exploring your relationships with those you love by visiting your past lives and life between lives is an exciting exercise. You discover the nature of your soul relationship with your loved ones, and whether you have incarnated with them before. You also discover that some of the issues causing trouble between you and the significant people in your life have arisen in previous incarnations. With increased understanding and strong determination, you are given an opportunity to resolve these issues.

The cases discussed in this chapter exemplify the emotional connections that can flow from one life to another or, as in the case of Lola, down the ancestral line. Some souls may invest many lifetimes in the same relationship, struggling to make it work. Others may draw powerful lessons from past relationships, whether they succeeded or failed. All our relationships can play out in myriad different ways. Everyone on the planet is unique and every relationship we have with others will reflect our individuality.

Creating relationships in which we respect ourselves and each other is not easy. Most people struggle to get this balance right. A regression can help when there are misunderstandings between people, and a need for more information. Knowing the past life history playing out in our relationships can give us the power and inspiration we need to take appropriate action—whether that action is to accept our life as it is, or to make radical changes.

Emotional Echoes

We create our own unhappiness. The purpose of suffering is to help us understand we are the ones who cause it.

WILLIE NELSON

Many people experience overwhelming emotions, such as anger, anxiety, grief and depression. While conventional therapies often help people address these emotions, there are times when they don't succeed. Many clients contact me because they haven't been able to locate the cause of their problems in their current lives. They sense, intuitively, that the answer lies somewhere beyond their current lived experience. This opens them to explore the possibility of past lives.

In the following cases, I explore the experiences of three clients who suffered from three common emotions: anxiety, anger and depression. Their sessions uncovered the root causes behind these emotions. Understanding these hidden causes helped my clients resolve their current emotional problems.

Anxiety

Dechen had been struggling with anxiety attacks for just over a year. She described her symptoms as heart palpitations, sweating, nausea, vomiting, diarrhea and a light, fluttery sensation in her head and chest.

Dechen worked at a hospital as a doctor. Her first anxiety attack occurred during a night shift. It hit her so intensely during her break that she had to go home. She said she had been strong and capable before the anxiety started. Her strength came, she explained, from her ability to block out anything too disturbing. She automatically detached from the suffering of distressed patients.

Now her anxiety was increasing and she started to identify with some patients, especially those who were anxious. Feeling out of control was uncomfortable and foreign to her. She had gone from feeling capable and resilient to having days when she felt so weak and vulnerable she couldn't go to work.

During our pre-brief she expressed her concerns concisely.

I'm afraid of something. Something inside that I'm afraid of bringing out. I feel stuck.

Dechen could not recall any specific incident that triggered her anxiety. She believed her anxiety was related to a past life. Before her session, we set the intention to experience a past life that would illuminate her current struggle with anxiety.

In the trance, Dechen found herself in seventeenth century England on a sunny but cool spring day.

The buildings are made of old, grey brick and I am in a place where people work. Today it is a market. Many people have come to the market to buy and sell. I am wearing a brown, clean but raggedy dress and worn, cloth shoes. My name is Lesandra. I am thirteen years old. I hope I can sell the vegetables I have grown. We need the money to pay the rent for the farm. And for other things.

I live with my father and younger sister. My mother died many years ago, after the birth of my sister. I look after the

74

house and do most of the cooking. The house is a little thatched cottage. I try to keep it clean and tidy. It is just one room. When it is cold, it is nice to be near the fire. Farming the land is hard and sometimes we struggle. At these times there is not a lot to eat. My father works hard on the farm. He is kind to me and my sister.

The next scene went right to the source of Dechen's anxiety.

It is early evening and I am tired after working hard in the garden. I fall asleep near the fire. Father has not yet returned home but my younger sister is there. I feel scared. Like something is going to happen.

There is a fire. I think my sister is cooking and spills something, maybe oil. It flares up. She doesn't know what to do and runs outside. The fire is spreading but I don't know. I suddenly wake. I am in a panic. So afraid. I try to get out. The fire is now roaring between me and the door. I am trapped. The smoke is suffocating me. I am going to die.

I gently help Dechen through the death of Lesandra. She cries.

Now I am above the fire and I can see my body. I feel sad. I was only sixteen. I want to say goodbye to my father and sister. They are distraught. They cannot see me but I know they feel a sense of comfort as I hug them.

Her guide appears, explaining that the stress and panic she experienced during the fire have been 'encapsulated'. This means the emotions associated with this disturbing event are repressed. Lesandra died suddenly, aged only sixteen. This devastated her and impacted her soul.

As Dechen, she senses that she cannot bear this deep emotional pain, so she avoids it. She is afraid to allow the full impact of these feelings into her body. So she disassociates from painful emotions. Her ability to block out disturbing emotions worked for many years, but holding back a dam of emotion takes a lot of energy. Eventually the load became too heavy and manifested as anxiety.

Releasing this stored emotion will take time, according to her guide. She needs to develop self-trust: trust that she can bear the disturbing emotions that will arise in her body and trust that she can let them go. The guide suggests she meditate. She needs to let the emotions come in rather than pushing them away.

I called Deshen several months later. She was happily pregnant and feeling fine. She said hadn't noticed any significant anxiety in recent times.

I have helped many clients resolve their anxiety after accessing a past life. One client, Barry, came to see me because he suffered from social anxiety. His anxiety was very specific. He only felt anxious whenever there were a few people around. With questioning, it became clear that the anxiety was at its worst when he was with two other people. He would become so nervous that he clammed up and couldn't interact.

To find the cause of the problem, I ask him to imagine being in this worst-case situation. At the same time, I assure him that he is safe. This gives him the confidence he needs to relive the experience. Once he is fully immersed in his anxiety, I suggest that he goes to its origin. I encourage him to go with whatever information surfaces.

Barry finds himself walking down a dirt road. He senses it is in America, more than 150 years ago. He is a free African American, barefoot and dressed in ragged clothes. He hears horses approaching. As he describes this scene, I see he is becoming more and more agitated and nervous. He tells me two white men come riding around a bend in the road. They pull up and start questioning him. It doesn't matter how hard he tries, nothing he says will placate them. Eventually, they grab a rope out of their saddlebags and throw it over a tree. There is nothing he can do. They seize him and string him up. They ride away, leaving him hanging there by the neck.

Barry seems to be stuck in the horror of this experience. Using a number of therapeutic techniques, I help him resolve this trauma. He weeps for several minutes, distressed at the suddenness and unfairness of the death.

Barry made another appointment but never came back. Instead he called to let me know his social anxiety had completely disappeared.

Here I have given you two extreme examples. Barry's anxiety was completely gone with just one relatively short, but tightly focused session. Dechen's anxiety was not fully released. She needed time to surface and release her fears and emotions.

Obviously anxiety can be released during a single session, but in Dechen's case her emotions had been deeply repressed. She was only able to free herself from her anxiety as she reflected on her experience, and allowed time to work its healing magic.

Anger

Terry was concerned with one thing, his anger. You briefly met

Terry before, in the chapter, *Proof.* He said he had been angry all his life. He vividly remembered feeling angry as a young boy while trying—unsuccessfully—to hammer nails into a piece of wood. In his frustration, he threw the hammer down.

He noticed that he reacted with intense fury to the thought of being betrayed. He hated any hint of hypocrisy. Compared to other people, he knew his reactions were way out of proportion. As soon as he woke in the morning, he felt irritated. He called it 'bubbling lava'. In the past three years, the bubbling lava had become unbearable. Both he and his wife had noticed increased moodiness, restlessness and shortness of temper.

Terry had spent a lot of time thinking about his life. Although he had experienced many incidents that had enflamed his anger, he could not point to a specific event that was responsible for all the rage he felt. He was convinced that the source of his anger came from a past life.

We embarked on the session with the clear intention to find the source of his anger and release it.

The sun lies low in the sky in the opening scene of Terry's past life. His name is Peter. He is wearing a long tunic over his trousers, and leather boots that sit high on his ankles.

I hear people talking behind me. I see a market lining a narrow, winding street that goes up the hill. It is medieval England. I am walking on cobblestones beside an old stone wall, looking for someone. I am full of anger. I am angry with the man I am seeking.

The road leads me towards a church. As I approach it I can feel my anger growing. Now, on the church steps, I see the man I've been looking for. He is dressed in black robes, like a monk. I am arguing with the monk. I did something for him, and it has not been appreciated.

I feel tall and strong and the monk seems small. I am standing over him. I tell him that he lied. His description of the mission was false. I have invested many years in this mission. I travelled many miles and went overseas to other countries.

I find myself speaking with Peter, rather than with Terry. I ask him to tell me about this mission.

I am on a horse riding with others to Jerusalem. I have a red cross on my tunic and others do too. We are going to fight for the One True Faith, Christianity.

I have left the farm where I lived. I had a life that was peaceful on that farm. I have been recruited into this war, persuaded by a monk. I am carrying a flag that is like a streamer, long and thin, red and white. Many men are here, some on horseback and some on foot.

We sail to France. Now we are walking through south-western France. I am striding alongside my horse most of the way. As we go along, many others join us. I can see a huge trail of dust stirred up by the feet of the men, the carts, and the hooves of the horses.

We are camped around a smoking fire. There are many tents, horses and people. It smells of unwashed bodies.

I am wondering why? We are near the fire looking at each other, wondering why we are taking this long, difficult journey. We are all damp and uncomfortable.

Now we are further along. It is cold and snowing. I see

that I am in the mountains, riding my horse over a mountain pass. Underneath my tunic I am wearing chainmail armour. There are people here who we have come to fight. I hear lots of screams and smoke and confusion.

I don't know where I am. I am coming down off a mountain. I see that the landscape is barren and rocky and studded with stunted trees. I can still hear the fighting behind me. In the distance we see an old walled city. We are trying to move towards this city.

Now I am inside the walled city. There are lots of ladies in grey, long dresses. They wear scarves over their heads.

I ask Peter if they are nuns.

No. They are not like nuns. I see from their faces that they are scared. We are wrecking their buildings and taking anything of value. We ride our horses through the street scaring them. I cannot see any men, only women and children. We are deliberately frightening anyone we see. If we can, we chase them away or knock them over with our horses. We destroy their homes and possessions for no reason. It is chaos.

I ask Peter if he or his comrades are killing people.

I don't see that. Just us damaging everything. I got caught up in it to start with but now I am ashamed. I am trotting slowly on my horse away from it all. My head is down. I feel so much shame. I can still hear lots of noise and confusion. I am trying to separate myself from it.

There is no one with me. I see a camel standing under a date palm. [He laughs.] *It seems strange. I haven't seen a camel before. I am looking at it from about twenty meters away. I am hot and thirsty and I go to this place where there is water. An oasis.*

I am standing on the edge of our camp. We are coming home. It all seems so pointless. We marched all that way and did all that damage for nothing. We were told that the purpose was Christianity. The One True Faith. But it doesn't make any sense. I am very confused. I was told we were going to do good things for a good purpose. But we just did bad things.

I am angry at being deceived. I am with the other soldiers. We are sitting around the campfire talking about it. We all feel the same. We have all been deceived. I can't wait to get home to confront the monk.

Now I am back in England, confronting the monk. He is waving his arms around and now he is walking away. I keep following him, pressing my point. We are on the side of the nave near a column. Oh. It feels like I got stabbed.

The monk has stabbed me in the stomach with a long, sharp, really thin dagger. He pushed it in and quickly pulled it out. I am looking down at the blood flowing from the wound onto my hand. I followed him into the church and he stabbed me. I have fallen to my knees and he is walking backwards away from me. He is running away. I am on my knees with a wound in my stomach. Dying.

As he watches Peter die, Terry starts crying quietly.

I am at peace. I am watching myself lying on the flagstones. I am glad it is all over. I can see the roof of a church and I can see through the roof to the sky above as well. I am floating upwards. Now I can see the city. There is a river. Now clouds. [He laughs.] *Clouds! I am floating through clouds. There is someone beside me. A feminine presence in a long dress. She is taking my arm and guiding me. I feel love.*

I am sitting on the grass in a park. It is beautiful with beautiful trees and colours. There are lots of people around. They are walking and talking. The woman is still there. It is warm and cool at the same time. So peaceful and calm. It feels like I am welcome.

The woman is my guide and she is right beside me. She is laughing. Her name is Gabrielle. I seem to be able to float. I don't have to walk. I can float!

I suggest we ask Gabrielle to explain the significance of Peter's life.

The purpose of my life as Peter was to experience separation and loss. To compare. To get a counterweight. We experience loss as well as connection so one can illuminate the other. It is to find the balance. Now she's whispering to me but I cannot hear her.

I suggest to Terry that he open up and be brave enough to hear what Gabrielle says. It might challenge his beliefs. He soon hears her and reports what she says. 'There is no God. Not the one you were taught was God.'

Terry breathes deeply and slowly, taking in Gabrielle's message. I give him time to regain his composure before asking about the similarities between the life of Peter and the life of Terry.

They are parallel lives. In both lives I wanted to do the right thing. I put my trust in people who tell me they have the truth but I end up being misled. I end up feeling betrayed. These people think they have the truth. They are passionate about their beliefs and I get caught up into it.

I get caught because I want the good things like peace and love and happiness. And I think that is what they are offering. But all they really want is power and control. They don't even know what they are doing. I can see through them now. There are many false prophets. Deceivers. That has made me very angry.

I ask what he needs to do to stop being caught up.

I know already. I need to trust my intuition.

To access my intuition, I need to be silent. I go searching in books and other places but the searching is not helpful. What I am searching for is here already. I have to sit quietly. I am not to listen to the words. My intuition is more than just words. It is a sense of knowing. I am being told that the information is there. I just need to tap into it.

I ask about the anger he has felt in these lives.

The anger I feel in each life is the same but the context is different. It is anger at being deceived…at allowing myself to be deceived.

These people who deceived me are supposed to be God's representatives. They are supposed to be the intermediaries between God and myself. Turns out they are not. And there is no God like we are taught. The concept of God, as it is taught, is used to control people.

Terry sighs deeply. 'Ah wow! I am feeling good.' He laughs. 'The penny has dropped.'

Some months after the session, Terry gives me an update.

Everything has changed completely. I came to you with anger issues. I wanted to find the cause of that anger. After I came back from overseas—including a visit to Turkey—I felt that I no longer fitted into my skin. Something had moved in me, and my body and I were no longer aligned. My search for answers accelerated.

I could see the parallels between that life and this life. The regression put it all together. Many pieces of the puzzle fell into place. I had trusted organised religion in this life too and been betrayed.

Three weeks after the regression I was sick one weekend. I had headaches, muscle aches and an upset stomach. I felt restless and disturbed. I guess that was the healing crisis. After that all the anger drained away. Now I feel unburdened and free. I feel more at peace now in my life than I ever have. Life is good.

Depression

Rachel[1] wants a regression because she is depressed. At times she thinks of suicide. She says she is feeling very lost and 'living the wrong life'. She has no partner and feels alone.

Her parents, she says, have conditioned her to be afraid of life. 'They have frozen me.' I wonder aloud if she thinks this might be the source of her depression, but she shakes her head. She

1 You will meet Rachel again in the chapter, *Soulmates*.

strongly senses that her feelings of being lost, alone and unhappy on the planet come from a past life.

She sets her intention for the session. She wants to experience a past life that helps her understand how to open to love.

When she arrives in the past life she is given two images. One is of a monk sitting on the ground meditating. The other is of dust and cowboys. I suspect we are going to be visiting two past lives. I ask her which image she would like to explore first. She chooses the meditating monk.

She describes a scene where the monk is sitting on the ground near a large tree. His head is shaved and he wears orange robes. Rachel approaches him. In this life her name is Tenzin. She is a female, also dressed in orange robes and wearing sandals. They are in a Japanese-style garden surrounded by pebbles, rocks, moss and bonsai trees in various arrangements.

Tenzin stands nervously in front of the meditating monk. She has to ask him something but doesn't want to disturb him.

I am worried that he might not like the question but I find the courage to ask: 'Do you know where Quan has gone? We can't find him.'

The Abbot has sent me to this meditating monk. I am definitely his junior. He is wise and I look up to him. He brought me to the monastery. Now I am a teacher. I vouched for Quan, but Quan has been naughty. He has run away again. The Abbot and the monk wanted to get rid of Quan but I didn't feel comfortable with that. I wanted to give him another chance. I thought if we were compassionate, Quan would come around and settle down. I am realising now that Quan has played me for a fool.

The monk smiles. He knows I am nervous but he loves me. I can see compassion in his eyes. I also see that he had known that Quan would go. He says I did the right thing when I vouched for Quan. I have also done the right thing coming to tell him Quan is missing.

I am relieved that the monk understands. But now I am nervous about going back to tell the Abbot that Quan is gone. I was wrong about Quan and I am always worrying about doing the wrong thing.

When I get there I feel fairly calm, thanks to the meditating monk.

The Abbot is impartial. He is not upset or angry. He said I did the right thing by telling him Quan is gone. He said showing compassion to Quan was good.

The Abbot says I need to be careful about people in the future. I can be naïve. I believe what people tell me. I take them at face value when they could have other agendas.

We go to another scene in this life as Tenzin. She is in a dark room surrounded with books and scrolls.

I was deeply disappointed with Quan. I really thought that showing love and compassion would change him. I never wanted to feel that disappointment again so I withdrew from going up the hierarchy. Before this happened I was very keen to progress. But after Quan, I didn't want to make any more decisions about people. I became a scholar. I wanted to deal with facts and words and not the messy human stuff. I never forgot Quan and how he fooled me.

We move on to the other life of dust and cowboys.

It is dusty in the wide main street in one of those frontier towns, the sort that has wooden platforms in the front of the stores instead of a sidewalk.

It is windy and hot. I am sweating. It's a gritty feeling.

I am a man named Johsua, dressed in black with black boots and a gun on my right hip. I am reaching for my gun. I am in an aggressive stance. There is someone lying on the ground a way off. I am moving towards him with my gun in my hand. He is on the ground because he fell. He was facing me and running backwards when he tripped. I can see he is terrified, and he should be. I am so angry, hurt and embarrassed, I want to kill him. Even though he is on the ground and isn't armed, I shoot him dead.

I know I am not going to get into trouble for this. I am in a bar drinking, while people are checking to see that I am fine. Some men are wary of me but most are friendly.

He was known to be dodgy. No one went to help him. He was not really a bad man. He was not a murderer or bank robber, just untrustworthy.

It is about money, a lot of money. I came from poverty but I wanted to be rich. I worked hard and made money through gold. I trusted this man and invested my money with him. He made me think I had a lot of money and it turned out I didn't. He lost it all.

There is woman involved. She comes up to me while I am in the bar. She is a very calming presence. She is sorry that now she can't be with me. She was going to be with me when I had money but now it cannot be. She comes from money.

My embarrassment arises from the way her father now

feels about me. He used to like me even though he doesn't usually mix with lower-class people. He accepted me when I was somebody who had money. We used to drink in nicer places than the bar I am in now. But now he cannot even look at me. He is not a bad man, he just lives in a different world.

When I found out that I had no money, I got angry. I shot the man who deceived me because I thought my life was over. Now I have nothing. That is not true, people like me. I am an amiable person. People laugh with me. I am easygoing.

But it is a hard world, especially without money. I am losing the girl too and we genuinely love each other. I trusted the wrong person.

We move to another scene.

I am in my forties. I am rich again and I am happy. I am married to a different woman and we have two children.

I have worked hard. A man, slightly older than me, cut me in on his business and gave me a chance. He trusted me and respected me. He knew I was a hard worker and honest. I own the business now. He didn't want the pressure but he still works there and makes money.

I still think about the original woman, Kate, who I miss, even though I love my wife. Kate represented success, hope, possibility and innocence. There was something I saw in Kate's eyes the last time she looked at me—a deep sense of loss and sadness.

I hang onto this image of her eyes and the feeling of loss. I hang onto it to remind me to be careful about who to trust.

I don't really let people in. I treat people well but I hold back, even with my children. I am not fully open. I have the walls up.

Rachel moves into observer mode as she continues to report on her life as Joshua.

Joshua has a deep sadness. That is his real honest emotion. He feels emptiness.

He has done everything he is supposed to do but he is still empty. He doesn't understand the point of things we humans have to do. He got on with life and threw himself into his business. But he feels it is not real. He wonders: 'What's the point? Why bother?'

Kate represented something real to him. After that he wasn't real anymore.

He has a deep inner grief. His wife knows it and it makes her sad and then he is sad sensing her sadness. He is a bit lost. Sometimes he feels like leaving it all.

He dies of old age in bed. He is a bit fat and with white hair. His children are sad. They love him.

He feels relieved to leave.

I feel his sadness, and the sadness of his family. He is sorry he couldn't open himself up to them. He feels he short-changed them.

Now he is going to die and the last thing he feels is regret. He realises that the most important thing is loving his family. He failed at that. He just couldn't get the walls down. He thinks he ruined his children's life a bit. Although he ticked all the 'good father' boxes, he was distant.

I encourage Rachel to feel her grief, giving her the time she needs to weep deeply. Grieving is essential if she wishes to heal her depression.

After she came out of the trance, Rachel knew she had more work to do—but she also knew she was on the right track to resolve her issues. She knew what unconditional love felt like. She felt that love from the serene monk who was so open and loving.

But she wasn't ready to forgive Joshua for being so distant. He reminded her of her own father, who did all the right things but never opened his heart to his children.[2]

As she reflected on the two past lives, she said, 'I am scared of getting hurt. Tenzin and Joshua blindly trusted everyone. They believed in the goodness of people. They had this naïve innocence.'

I suggest that sometimes innocence can be dangerous. Rachel replies, 'But innocence is so beautiful.'

I know Rachel is coming back to explore the realms in her life between lives and I trust her naïve innocence will be balanced during that regression.

Rachel sent me an email soon after her session saying she feel much happier and lighter. Her depression had lifted.

Discussion

These three cases provide evidence that emotional problems in our current lives can originate in previous lives. However, I do not rule out the possibility that emotional issues surface from trauma in our current life. I have had clients who found themselves bogged down in childhood trauma during a session, when

---

2 Refer to Rachel's life between lives in the chapter *Soulmates* to see how her feelings change.

they expected to be visiting a past life. These clients had difficult childhoods with issues they had carried into adulthood. Later we discovered that some of their problems did have their genesis in traumatic past lives. However, it seems their guides decided that childhood issues needed to be resolved first, because that is where they were taken during the regression.

How do you tell if your issues have come from this life or a past life? If you have tried different therapies without success, it may indicate that the source of your problems lies deeply buried. By the time they decided on a regression, each of the clients you met in this chapter had a strong sense that their problems came from previous lives.

Dechen had been to several counsellors before undertaking her session. Even though these counsellors had used various therapies, they had not been able to fully resolve Dechen's anxiety. Through regressing to a past life, she learned that her anxiety was the result of fearful emotions that had been deeply repressed. Her guides suggested that regular meditation would bring any unresolved emotions to the surface and it did.

Barry, on the other hand, resolved his anxiety after only one session. Reliving the horror and injustice of his lynching and coming to terms with his sudden death freed him from his fears.

The anger that Terry had been struggling with all his life was resolved by his regressing to his past life. Terry was in his late fifties and perhaps the timing was just right. He was really ready to let it go. His session began a healing process that ended his over-reactive anger.

Rachel received relief from her deep depression. In her case too, the session began a process of resolution.

The past lives discussed in this chapter played an important role in helping each client understand the nature of his or her emotional problems. However, the session was only the start of the changes. Even though Dechen was told what had created her anxiety, this was mostly an intellectual understanding. She still needed to sit with her emotions and fully release her fears.

Both Terry and Rachel also had to continue healing after they received information about their issues.

Visiting our past lives can help us discover the source of many emotional issues and also play a significant role in resolving our problems such as depression, anger and anxiety.

Healing

Every human being is the author of his own health or disease.
SWAMI SIVANANDA SARAWATI

Although I am specifically focusing on clients with health issues in this chapter, nearly all clients experience some aspect of healing. Even people who undertake a regression out of curiosity can reap the healing benefits of their experience. Pattie, who you met in an earlier chapter, received confirmation that she was on track with her life. Although such a change is subtle, she was healed of any doubts about her direction, enabling her to approach her life with renewed vigor.

Some people, however, do suffer from pain or serious health issues. Usually they want to know why they have these health issues, and what they can do to reduce their suffering.

Here are some cases of people who were facing a range of health challenges. I have also included more general information and suggestions that the Council of Elders have given to people with health issues.

Morris[1]

Morris is only in his thirties but he has already experienced a rare cancer. He had undergone several rounds of chemotherapy and the cancer had gone into remission. However his doctor was still

---

1 You will discover more about Morris in a later chapter, *Body Selection*.

concerned, and Morris was about to have more tests. His doctor had flagged the possibility he might need another round of chemotherapy. Morris was not sure if that would be wise.

For his current life, Morris had chosen a sensitive body that was prone to illness. In the chapter, *Body Selection*, you will discover the reasons behind his choice.

During his session, Morris asked the Council of Elders for advice on how to manage his body. He was told he had two choices. He could remain incarnate, or he could leave. The Council advised him of the steps he needed to take if he wished to heal.

Be careful with toxins and make sure you detox regularly. You need to detox emotionally, spiritually and physically. This means keeping the energy flowing. Beware of emotional and energy blockages.

Your body is sensitive to illness and also sensitive to healing. You can heal yourself. You need to meditate and tap into a higher consciousness. If things haven't gone too far, the body can be healed.

All healing is possible but if the body has been damaged [such as cartilage destroyed in a joint] *then you need a stronger intent. You need to believe in your healing one hundred percent. You have to have no doubts.*

Meditate, visualise, feel the healing, feel healed, bring the healing into being. Whether you use medicine to reduce the pain or not, the main thing is to not get into the fear.

Those who act healthy and feel healthy are healthy.

When the Council referred to toxins, they were not just talking about unhealthy food or poisons (such as chemotherapy) taken into the body. The Council was also referring to toxic people. Around the time that Morris had developed the cancer, he had experienced a year of conflict. This conflict occurred within his extended family when a relative embarked on a path of fraud and deception. Some members of the family were taken in by this man, while others were not. The conflict split the family apart. Morris and his wife had recently emigrated to get away from all the tension.

Steven

Steven is in his sixties. He is a health professional who has helped many people. Sheer curiosity led him to seek out a regression. He mentioned that he was on dialysis for kidney failure. He was generally very accepting of this physical challenge, saying he had found ways to get on with his life in spite of the illness. He was not seeking a cure but he wondered why he had fallen ill. During the session, he was given his answer.

> *I chose my kidney failure. I get the feeling I had to clear out all the shit I was carrying. I had cruel parents. Even though, through their cruelty and pain, I learned about love. The kidney failure has made me more patient and tolerant. I have to go on dialysis every few days and sit for hours. It is an interesting disease. You know you are terminal, but not yet. I am being told that feeling unwell will come and go. My journey is to experience many possibilities. It is just another experience. The most important thing is to enjoy the journey. I will not let* [my illness] *bother me.*

At a soul level, Steven chose his illness because it presented a challenge. It seems that many souls choose such challenges. What he learned during his session confirmed this for Steven and helped him make peace with his illness.

Elyssa

Elyssa was very depressed and sometimes indulged in self-harming behavior. She wondered what she needed to do to change her unhappiness.

Early in our discussion before the regression, I noticed the rigidity of her views. During the session, her rigidity turned to resistance. She kept saying she thought she was making it all up. Somehow, this notion filled her with fear—a fear that knowing she was making it up would only deepen her depression. But as we proceeded further into the trance, she was given information to help her change.

> *I create my reality. I know that is true. I have to give up my limiting beliefs to be able to create a better reality. I am very negative. I don't think I am good enough. This is coming from my thought patterns. My father's treatment of me is part of it. My father was a blamer. His father was a blamer. My mother's family was full of blamers. This victim attitude has come down the ancestral line.*
>
> *One part of me wants to change and another part doesn't. The resistant part wants to stay as it is because it feels familiar. I can feel it in my body. My neck is tense and painful.*
>
> *I am being told to open up, make space, expand and allow the feelings to be in my body.*

Elyssa started crying quietly and continued to cry for some time as she worked through those generations of blame and grief.

I can see that sad little me that I was. I can feel her sadness… I am giving it space… Now I am holding her hand. I feel at peace with this reconnection.

I am being told I am to be much more gentle with myself. I need to be less negative. I can do this by accepting the negativity and giving it space. I am to do what I sense is right for me and not to worry about what anyone else thinks.

Elyssa felt greatly drained after this session, but she was on her way to increased self-acceptance and reduced negativity. She could heal her depression and self-harming behavior if she continued to practise what she had been given.

Lionel

Lionel was extremely overweight and suffered a number of other illnesses due to this. His doctors pointed to his weight as the main problem. He wanted to know why he struggled so much with food and what he could do about it.

One of his past lives is described in the chapter, *Do Our Past Lives Affect This Life?* In that life he lived as a noble, using food as a weapon to control his peasants. He hated the injustice of some people having more than others, even though he was born into wealth.

He experienced a previous life in a Nordic country around 800 A.D. where food again was an issue.

In this Nordic life, he was a woman who struggled to find enough to eat. She built up a lot of anger over the injustice of a few having so much and the peasants having so little. She and her husband intended to steal from a wealthy man. However, their intended victim failed to arrive at their carefully-chosen place of ambush, and so their plan was aborted. She never tried to steal again, even though starving remained a threat throughout this life. She had children and sometimes she went hungry in order to feed them.

In another past life, Lionel was an intelligent man who rose to great power. He governed a large area of a third world country and did as much as he could to support the masses. But he died disillusioned. He felt he could have done more even though the people were grateful for what he did.

The theme of injustice for the poor and underprivileged ran through all of these lives. In his current life, Lionel still harbours a strong sense of injustice. He is certainly not privileged in this life as he struggles financially, mainly due to limited work opportunities and his poor health.

During the session, Lionel remembered a time when he was six years old and attending a birthday party for one of his friends. Even though he was only six, he had been putting on weight. He had recently started cutting back on fattening food. At this party, he refused to eat chocolate, lollies or ice-cream and was quite at peace with his choice. He overheard one of the mothers commenting positively on his ability to be so strong and determined. This was a powerful memory. The Council of Elders referred to this memory when advising him how to heal his relationship with food.

The Council said that fundamentally his problem lies in his tendency to see food as offering something other than sustenance. Lionel also uses food to fill his deeper emotional needs, such as the need for punishment, rebellion, comfort and so forth.

He is told that healing is difficult because there are many subtleties involved from many past lives. However, the Council tells Lionel that if he wishes to heal, he needs to use food purely for sustenance—even though he is not fully aligned with that idea yet. This is an area where he needs to continue to challenge himself.

His body is very confused. His appetite is distorted and his stomach doesn't know when it is full. He doesn't know what he really needs to eat. Over time, however, as he eats healthily his body will learn these positive new habits, and the old symbolic connections will disappear. There are many resources available that will help him know what to eat and what not to eat. It may challenge him but it is the correct way to proceed.

Cecily

Cecily has a brain tumor that is being treated with radiation and chemotherapy. She wants to know why the tumor formed, and how she can help heal it.

When she regresses to her past life, Cecily discovers she was married to a physically abusive alcoholic. She has carried over hurt and anger from this life. In her present life, her alcoholic father neglected her, paying more attention to his sons than his daughter. Then her husband left her a couple of years before she was diagnosed with the tumor. This compounded the trauma.

Cecily takes this knowledge into her life between lives. She encounters some wise beings, who explain that tumors represent 'an accumulation of dense energies', including the hurt and trauma experienced over many lifetimes.

Cecily connects with her grief, crying deeply for several minutes. She forgives her father for his neglect, realising he didn't know how to interact with a daughter. He was rough with the boys but kept his distance from her, because he didn't want to injure her.

The wise beings explain that illness is useful, because anything the body does is useful. It is a feedback mechanism that tells us what is going on in our psyche. Tumors represent an opportunity to evolve, 'a gift of lifetimes,' they say. I ask what is meant by 'a gift of lifetimes' and the wise beings reply:

> *Tumors accumulate from lifetimes of experience. When they manifest in your life, you are given the opportunity to understand the path you have taken. Then you can heal the trauma and let it go.*
>
> *With any illness, you need to identify the space and time when the trauma was locked in the body. Sit with the ill part of the body focus on it, talk with it and listen so you can understand what it says. Then to help heal illness, visualise it, sense its essence and make peace with it, while at the same time being non-judgmental and accepting.*

Fighting the illness, fighting anything that the body creates, is not useful.

Eddie

Eddie is disabled. When he was young, he had an accident that left him a paraplegic. Before this happened, he was an athlete and into extreme sports.

After his accident, Eddie didn't grieve his loss, not for long anyway. He distracted himself from grief and loss by focusing on what he could achieve, rather than on his disability. As he felt comfortable playing sport, he became a wheelchair basketball player, and worked his body hard. Everyone admired his strength of character.

His new focus served him well until he had another accident, this time during a game. The doctors thought he might end up a quadriplegic. He didn't, but while this remained a possibility, Eddie lay in bed thinking. He wondered why the accidents had happened to him. Being told it was 'God's will' didn't satisfy him. The question became an obsession, and he started looking for answers. Eventually, he heard about life between lives regression.

During the session, he discovers his disability was part of the plan for his current life. He is in the process of developing balance between the physical and non-physical. Some people over-identify with their body, ignoring their spiritual connection. Others focus on the spiritual realms, resisting their physical nature and the realities of our physical world. At an advanced stage of development, souls set out to balance these two contrasting attractions.

Eddie is told he needs to spend time meditating, focusing on his inner world, as well as staying fit and playing sport. This will allow him to find the balance he seeks.

The wise beings explain that many disabilities are planned before we are born, to help the individual grow in some way. For example, being born visually impaired bestows opportunities not available to sighted people. By looking within, blind people can develop their intuition. Their listening skills and their feeling sense are also greatly enhanced.

Mark

Mark came to see me because he was feeling emotionally attacked by his ex-wife, complaining that she has never supported him or the children. He is very successful in his career and his new marriage is happy, but his ex-wife is jealous. In her bitterness, she told lies to their teenage children and turned them against him.

He struggled with a major setback in his career at the same time his children became spiteful towards him. Then, his mother was diagnosed with a terminal illness. Mark always endeavours to be positive but he was finding it difficult to maintain the act. Underneath he was feeling a tremendous amount of stress. He was self-doubting and negative. Soon after all the stress, he began losing his hearing.

In his life between lives, he is told his negativity caused his hearing problems.

> *Your negative self-talk and high expectations of yourself are the reasons you lost your hearing. You didn't want to hear the negativity anymore. If you want to stay healthy, you must stop the negative self-talk and continue meditating. You are burning off a lot of karma by your daily meditation. Keep doing that and your health will improve and stay improved.*

Mark received other useful advice about reconnecting with his children and letting go of his anger at his ex-wife. He left confident that his health would improve, and feeling more at peace with his situation.

Conclusion

Healing appears to be automatic when we are in the realm of our life between lives. As soon as we arrive, we are taken to a center where all heaviness and pain is released. One soul, in his life between lives, was clearly given this message.

When you visit this sacred place, you are cleared of all negativity. You cannot be in this scared place with negativity. Here there is clarity and purity. You choose what you take back to Earth with you. You return cleansed and pure and you need to remain vigilant so you continue to instill clarity and purity into your thoughts and body.

Unfortunately, when we return to Earth after being in our life between lives, some of us pick up our old patterns. Perhaps it takes a very strong soul to permanently wash away the old destructive negativity that we seem to hold in our bodies.

The next time I spoke with Morris about his struggle with cancer, he told me that he felt fine. Eventually though, his doctor persuaded him that another round of chemotherapy would be useful to keep the cancer under control. Morris had acquiesced. Although I recalled his guides suggesting he be wary of toxins, I said nothing and wished him the best. A few years later, his wife contacted me. Morris had passed.

Some of the clients in this chapter were able to instill their new learnings into their physical bodies. Elyssa, for example, continued to work with the information she was given in her session. Her health, her relationships and her life improved and she described herself as happy.

Spirit guides tell us healing is possible. We need to change our mindset from pain to comfort, from fear to trust, and from negativity to positivity. Specifically, they said, 'Those who act healthy and feel healthy, are healthy.'

I decided to implement this advice to address my own health problem. My right hip was so damaged that a specialist said I needed a hip replacement. I had been in pain with this hip for years and I was now only walking when I had to. It had worsened over the last two years and I even used a wheelchair for long distances when I was overseas. I realised that as I walked, I focused on the pain. This is understandable, given that pain seems to cry out for attention. I gave it attention—negative attention.

When I decided to take the guides' advice, I focused attention on my pain-free left hip, enjoying the freedom of movement in that leg as I walked. Then I imagined my right hip feeling that same freedom. To help, I also mentally repeated the words, 'strength and comfort' as I walked.

Whenever I did this, I noticed that the pain in my right hip and leg reduced significantly. Often, I walked without pain. Sometimes I would forget, feel some pain, and fall into my old habit of tightening up against the discomfort.

I managed sufficiently for another three years after the surgeon said I should have my hip replaced. During that time, there were two major improvements in hip surgery that helped make my new hip durable, my operation successful, and my recovery swift.

Facing Death

For what is it to die, but to stand naked in the wind and to melt into the sun? ...And when the Earth shall claim your limbs, then you shall truly dance.

KAHLIL GIBRAN

We all die, whether we want to or not. The idea of dying can be challenging, even for those who believe that we survive the death of the physical body.

While in a physical body, we naturally focus on material things—our safety, our pursuits, our possessions, our interactions with others, the beauty of our world and its challenges. When we die, the world we knew is gone. The people we cherished are out of reach. If we are not prepared, death is a shock.

Some people never face the fact that they and their loved ones will die. I have counselled people overwrought by the death of a greatly loved, elderly pet. They had never considered this day would come. I wondered why they were so unprepared. I eventually worked it out. They hated loss and were not good at letting go. The thought of losing a pet was so traumatic, they never thought about it. Pushing away the thought was easier than being prepared. Of course, the day of loss came anyway, and their lack of preparation meant that it hit them extremely hard.

This lack of preparedness does not apply just to the loss of pets. Many people avoid thinking about their own death or the death of their loved ones. When they are faced with a profound loss, these are the people who say, 'I never thought this would happen to me.' Previously, when someone they knew died, they had managed to distance themselves from their emotions. Now they cannot. The loss is too great.

Facing death takes courage. Some people have the fortitude to face death well before the grim reaper knocks on their door. This is wise. Although one can never be fully prepared, much of the fear of death can be resolved beforehand.

People who undertake past life or life between lives regressions often lose their fear of death. This happens for two reasons. First, they experience dying in their past lives. Second, they discover where they go after death.

Pattie, whose past lives are described in the chapter, *Not Cleopatra*, did not have any expectations from her session. She was just curious. But she did get something she never anticipated.

And the other thing I got that surprised me was a sense that, when I die in this lifetime, there is nothing much to fear. My energy was really positive and swirling and dancing up above, just after both lifetimes, just after dying. Death is easy if you let go gently.

Genevieve

Genevieve claimed she was not afraid of death but she was afraid of being at home alone at night. She had always wanted to visit the other side and now she had the opportunity. A relative gifted her a past life regression and a life between lives regression.

Before we proceed into the past life, Genevieve says she has a sore stomach. Genevieve regresses easily, staying one step ahead of me in my role as hypnotherapist. Her first past life soon reveals the reason for her stomach pains.

It is night-time and I am inside. It is cold and dark. I can see out of the windows. There are pink spots like eyes moving. Now it is getting lighter. There is a light near my face. I can see green trees.

I don't think I am alive. I don't think I have a body. I see a big eye again looking at me. I feel very little. My stomach hurts.

They're stabbing swords into my stomach. I am lying on a table in an old castle. My mother is standing at the end of the table. As terrible as it is, I am not going to cry. I will not give them the satisfaction.

But now Genevieve does cry, and takes some deep slow breaths. It takes a few minutes for her to release the pain in her stomach and the emotions associated with the horror of it all. Now she receives more information about this life.

My name is Mary and I am dressed all in white. This is a time after the Romans, in England. The castle is by the sea in the south of England.

I was naughty. I am the King's daughter and I fell pregnant to a man who is good to me but he is not acceptable to my mother. He was the gardener. We loved each other. The King's men came dressed in armour to kill me.

My father ordered my death because my mother wanted me killed. They wanted to show that poor guy not to mess with the King. I am above his station. They hanged him.

My mother in my current life was also Mary's mother.

This issue about class difference has carried into my current life. My mother never approved of my two partners. She never thought they were good enough for me. She has never let go of being the queen, even in her current life. My dad and his sister call her Queen Ann. Ann is her name. She carries on so much that my partner mockingly calls my family 'blue bloods'.

My father then is a different soul to my father now. Mary's father killed a lot of people to get the land so others wouldn't take them over.

Genevieve's guide is with her and we ask about the purpose of her life as Mary.

I was trying to set a precedent. I wanted to show that poor people can mix with the rich. I was a fighter. I was trying to stand up for myself, and others. I did what I thought was right for everybody, not just me.

(In a later regression, we discover Mary was a wilful soul, who was out of alignment with the era in which she lived. The guides explain that there is a time for change and a time to accept the circumstances of life. When you are open and connected to your higher self, you know which direction to take.)

Before Genevieve transitions into another past life she says, 'I don't know why I try to punish myself.' Again she is foreseeing the next step, as we discover.

Something is not right. I am being punished again.

I see tangled vines circled around me. I am in white, a Victorian dress to just below the knees with long sleeves and hemmed with lace. I am a ten-year-old girl called Sarah and I am crying.

I have run away and I am lost. My eye is hurting because I have been hit by my twelve-year-old brother. He hit me after I yelled at one of our servants, an old lady who is actually quite kind.

I am the daughter of the family who lives in a big, old stone house near the sea in England. I ran away because I knew I would be in trouble for being rude to the servant.

I can see the family all dressed up, the men with top hats. They are leaving in carriages to go to a funeral. I wanted to go too but I wasn't allowed. I was angry and I took it out on the old lady who stayed home to look after my brother and me. It is my grandmother's funeral. I wanted to go and say goodbye. I am upset because I loved my grandmother. That's why I ran away.

No one comes to get me because they can't find me. It is so dark and scary, I am afraid to leave. I don't know how to get home so I stay there and just cry.

Men in uniforms find me in the morning, the police I think. I can't stop crying.

They take me home and everyone is cross with me for being so silly. I think I gave my mother a nervous breakdown but my father is nice. My brother is nasty, laughing at me and calling me a spoilt brat.

No one is interested in why I did it. They don't understand, thinking I was just being naughty. Not being able to say goodbye to my grandmother has clung to me.

My brother is listening to me now, saying different people show their sadness in different ways. That feels nice.

We move to another scene in Genevieve's life as Sarah.

Now I am fourteen and we are leaving England on a big boat bound for Australia. Father has a high role on the ship but he is not the captain. We [his family] are allowed to go along. There is a tutor on board for us and the other children. We will be returning to England, but the other passengers will be staying in Australia.

We arrive in Darwin. The ship moors in the ocean and we come ashore in a small boat. As we get off, we have to watch for crocodiles. Some people will be settling here, mostly government workers and their families. There is not much to see, just a few old timber houses and some Chinese and Aboriginal people. There are not many white folk but we visit a few. They are all really scared of the Aboriginal people.

We move to another scene, discovering that Sarah and her family continued on to Cairns.

I am fifteen now and I am with another family travelling out into the bush. I am happy because it is an adventure. I have been allowed to stay with this family as a nanny to their children.

The previous nanny was their grandmother and she died. I felt sorry for the children losing their grandmother. I know how that feels, and wanted to look after them. The father is a government officer and we are going to the gold fields. It is scary, all bush and no roads. We have to find a way through.

We arrive at the goldfields and live in a timber house. Someone who hates the government sets it alight. It burns down and we all die. I am only sixteen.

I die peacefully. It was quick.

My parents are in Sydney and they just found out that I have died. They are sorry I went with that group. Mother is shouting at father. She is saying he shouldn't have let me go. I want to interrupt her. I want to tell her that I'm fine because I've been reunited with my grandmother. Somehow, I cut through her suffering. I see her face relax. She apologises to my father. They're still sad but they feel more at peace.

They decide to settle in Sydney. I think they are my maternal grandmother's family in my current life.

Genevieve now reflects on the deaths she has just experienced in these two past lives.

This death is strange. It seems awful to be burnt to death but it wasn't. Sarah's death was so different to the death of Mary. Mary was fighting death. Sarah didn't know she was dying. She fell asleep and died. Then her grandmother was there and it was fine. Sarah missed her grandmother so much she didn't mind dying.

Genevieve's two deaths are worth examining. Both were horrible ways for a sixteen-year-old to die, but there is one major difference. Mary's death involved her parents. The very people who are supposed to protect her had ordered her to die. As a result, Mary never accepted her death. She remained stoic, refusing to cry out, angry at the injustice she perceived. Mary clung tightly to those emotions as she died.

Sarah, on the other hand, did not resist her death. She missed her grandmother, who was there to meet her when she died. She was fully resolved at the time of her death. In fact, she made some effort to reassure her parents that she was fine before she left the Earth's sphere.

Before her session, Genevieve had told me that she was afraid of being alone at night, especially when all the lights were off. I decide I will test Genevieve now and see if resolving Mary's death has reduced her fear of the dark. I ask Genevieve to imagine being in her house alone when it is dark.

It is dark and scary. I can hear conversations. People are talking. They are outside. Oh. They're spirits. Actually, they are the spirits of Indigenous people. They are restless. You know, Murdering Creek is just near us, at the back of our house.

Murdering Creek got its name from a massacre that took place there about 150 years ago. A white man dressed as a swagman enticed the local Gubbi Gubbi people out of their lakeside camp to follow him along the lake and up the creek. Seven white men were lying in wait, holding their rifles. When their victims came within range, the whites opened fire. They fired again on those who fled. No one knows how many were killed. Unfortunately, this was not the only massacre of Indigenous people around these parts of the Sunshine Coast at that time.

I encourage Genevieve to send out a beam of light and love from her heart to these Indigenous spirits. I suggest she continue doing this until she knows she has their attention.

They are crying. I am sending light and love to them. They are aware of me now. I can read their minds and they are wondering if they can take their possums with them?

I tell Genevieve to send them the message that they can take their possums. She should also ask them to look for the elders who can guide them. I suggest she watch what happens next.

They were lost. They took the possums with them for food. They are going up into a golden light. Gosh, there are a lot of them. Hundreds... They are gone now.

I contact Genevieve six weeks after her session to see how she is going. She reports that she is much less fearful and no longer afraid of the dark. Funny thing, she cannot remember the lost Indigenous souls and their possums. In fact, she has little memory of anything that happened in the session. Our conversation takes place just a couple of days after Christmas. She has guests and it is the holidays. No doubt she has more practical things on her mind.

I speak with Genevieve again a month after Christmas. By now she has taken the time to listen to the recording of her session. Being home alone at night no longer frightens her. She also remarks that the possums that had made such a terrible nuisance of themselves around her house have gone, never to return. She says she hadn't connected all those dots until she listened to the recording of her regression.

Nicole

Nicole was another person who had a fear of being alone at night. She came to see me because of her anxiety. Many situations bothered her but being alone at night was looming as a major problem. Nicole's husband had been promoted and needed to attend a meeting interstate. For the first time in her twenty-four years, Nicole was going to be alone for several nights.

After making sure Nicole feels safe and secure, I regress her back to a time when she was home alone. I ask her to access her fears.

> *I am in the house and I feel afraid. Are all the doors locked? Can anyone get in? I am afraid someone might break in and hurt me. I cannot relax. I am walking up and down the hall checking everything. I hear sounds. Oh! It is just the neighbours putting out the rubbish. I am so jumpy any noise worries me.*

I know that the best way to transcend fear is to confront it. This situation of being alone has triggered Nicole's underlying fears. Now that the fear has surfaced, she has the opportunity to put it to rest.

Her greatest fear is that she would die. She bravely says she wants to confront this fear and release it.

Nicole believes in past lives so it is easy to remind her that she cannot die, not permanently anyway. Reassurance settles her a little. However, *believing* you never really die is not the same as *knowing* you survive death.

Nicole still feels anxious. I ask what she fears might happen. She says she is afraid someone will come in and murder her. I suggest we press *pause* for a moment so she can process what she is experiencing.

A man has broken in. He rapes me and now he has his hands around my neck. He is strangling me and I cannot stop him. I am struggling. I don't want to die. I am too young to die.

I agree by telling Nicole that our physical bodies do die, and when that happens our life, as we knew it, is over. She is angry. She doesn't think it is fair to have to die so young.

I encourage Nicole to feel her anger and disappointment, suggesting she go with any emotions that emerge.

When she is calm, I suggest we move forward again. She needs to accept death and let go. I keep reassuring her as she moves through the grief of her life's end.

I don't know if I can let go. I don't want my life to end. I had many things I wanted to do. I don't know where I am going. I am afraid. I am letting go now. I can see my body. It doesn't seem right that we have to die. That is a horrible way to die. [Nicole weeps.] I am letting go. Moving now…faster. I am being pulled backwards, upwards through a tunnel. The earth is far away. I can see a light up ahead and I am being pulled towards it. Now I am floating through crystal raindrops. So beautiful. I can feel the light. It is all around me, so warm and loving.

Tears roll down Nicole's cheeks. I suggest she stays awhile in this place that feels so warm and safe.

Nicole smiles. She tells me that she feels at peace. She is not alone, and feels surrounded by love. I ask her if she remembers how she reached this peaceful place.

She tells me that she travelled through a tunnel.

I ask her what happened before she went through the tunnel. Her voice fills with wonder.

I died! I was scared in the house and someone came in. They strangled me. Ohhh. That is so strange. Once I let go I went into that beautiful place of peace. I remember the crystal raindrops and the love. There is so much love.

When Nicole meets her guide, she wants to know why we have to live and then die.

He is telling me it is our own choice to come into a life. He says we choose our death, too. That seems strange. I am asking him why I would choose to die like that. It is to balance. To understand. We have to experience both. What we do in one life to others we have to experience too. Then we know and that is how we heal. He says we do not need to be afraid of death. All the pain melts away. In the end we are all loved and accepted.

A smile forms on Nicole's face. When I bring her out of the trance, we talk for a few minutes before I ask her to close her eyes and imagine she is back in her house alone.

'How do you feel?' I ask her.

'Much better,' she replies.

'Is there anything to be afraid of?'

'No. It is quiet and really peaceful'. She opens her eyes and starts laughing.

There is no reason to be afraid. Wow! All that worry I had and there is nothing to really be afraid of. I can remember that feeling of love, so warm and...comforting. Knowing what is waiting, it is hard to be afraid of death.

Conclusion

When someone dies unprepared or traumatically, the emotion associated with death might remain unresolved. I base this view on the hundreds of clients I have regressed, who have metaphorically 'died' as part of the experience. During their session, they release any emotional trauma or shock associated with the death. I have observed that their anxiety, fear or stress is nearly always relieved, never to return.

Some popular movies such as *Ghost* and *The Sixth Sense* have explored the theme of earthbound souls. In *Ghost*, the soul is focused on resolving his sudden death. In *The Sixth Sense*, the psychologist does not know he is dead.

Although these movies are dramatised to entertain their audience, they show how souls could be trapped in the Earth system. The energy that is trapped is not complete and the soul's focus is very limited. In *The Sixth Sense*, the young psychic schoolboy says that these dead people 'only see what they want to see'. My experience tells me that this description is apt. Genevieve, as Mary, did not have a peaceful death. She was horrified at being murdered on the instructions of her parents. At the moment of death, she was focused on the negativity of this experience. Such focus, I believe, traps the negative emotion that can reverberate in future lives. Perhaps Genevieve was guided to access this past life in order to release this negative emotional energy.

One of the benefits of regressing to our past lives and life between lives is the opportunity to release unneeded emotional energies, whether these energies are from a disturbing past life or a traumatic death.

A number of professionals have investigated the phenomenon of lost souls. In his book, *Thirty Years Among the Dead*, Dr. Carl Wickland describes how he rescued hundreds of dead people with the help of his psychic wife. Dr. William Baldwin, in his book, *Spirit Releasement Therapy*, considers the predicament of earthbound souls and outlines techniques for releasing them. Dr. Edith Fiore (*The Unquiet Dead*) and Dr. Louise Ireland-Frey (*Freeing the Captives*) also claim to have released many lost souls.

Many religions, traditional and primitive, have prayers and rituals to release the spirits of the dead. Perhaps we should not ignore the importance of a peaceful death.

How can we ensure we have a peaceful death, no matter what the circumstances? Prepare. Attaining an attitude of acceptance is the best preparation. When death looms, even unexpectedly, it only takes a split-second to release and let go.

A regression can be a positive experience for those who fear death. It is difficult to retain this fear if you have experienced death, even if it took place in a trance. Dying, and then finding blissful peace, is a powerful accomplishment. Something deep inside us changes. I know I no longer feel afraid of dying. Instead, I imagine dying with a sense of peaceful acceptance. When the reaper arrives, surrender now seems easy. Many others, who have visited a past life or their life between lives, express similar sentiments.

My Life's Purpose

You Can't Always Get What You Want
LIFE, ACCORDING TO THE ROLLING STONES

Most people would like to know what they are meant to be doing with their lives. During my twenty years of counselling, I have noticed that people are unsettled and unhappy if they sense they are not fulfilling their life's purpose.

A visit to their life between lives gives people the opportunity to discover their life's purpose. During their session, they receive much more than just information. Usually they relive a primary past life in their first session, and a secondary past life during the life between lives session. All these experiences, as well as the challenges they face in their current lives, provide fodder for examination. Their guides and the Council of Elders help them understand, first hand, the themes that are playing out in their lives. People come to see that the challenges, the events and the people in their current lives are there for a reason. As one client put it, 'I felt I had been given the missing piece of the puzzle about why I behaved the way I did, and why I was who I was.'

When I conduct these sessions, I make only one firm promise: *you will get what you need*. Occasionally someone who expected to experience a past life does not. They go the trance but other issues come up that need to be addressed. Even though their expectations were not fulfilled, they leave happy. Their guides know exactly what they need. Their guides have brought them to my consulting room for a reason. That reason unfolds, and, by the time the session is over, the client has gained some valuable insights to take away.

Most people think that their life's purpose is a job or a specific career. This is rarely the case. As you will see in the following stories, our purpose is more about refining the quality of our consciousness than the type of work we do. The physical skills we develop during our life die with the body, because the body is the vehicle for these skills. Our guides have described these physical abilities as 'tools'. Fortunately, spiritual lessons do seem to carry over from life to life. These lessons are essential to our ongoing spiritual evolution.

Many of my clients have been the victims of violence in their past lives. Others have acted violently themselves. They usually find these memories challenging. To help them make sense of these experiences, I often ask them, 'Do you now have any desire to kill another human?' They never do, of course. Then I ask, 'Did you have that desire earlier in your life, before learning better?'

They answer, 'No. I have always felt that way. I have never wanted to hurt anyone.'

Then I ask, 'So where did that knowing come from? Others in our world have the desire to kill. You don't. And most likely you couldn't, even to save yourself.' They cannot answer. They don't know how they developed such a distaste for violence.

I suspect they lost any desire to kill others through the experience of many lifetimes, lifetimes where they were killed and lifetimes where they killed. Once they have experienced both sides of the coin, so to speak, the desire to kill melts away. They know how it feels to be a victim and don't want to inflict that on another.

This entropy of the killing instinct is, in my view, a change in consciousness that stays with us, once it is fully integrated into our psyche or soul. We improve the quality of our consciousness through many experiences that are eventually integrated. What we experience during the life between lives session, is a shift in our understanding. As we reflect on that experience it is integrated into our consciousness. Once we understand our journey, we know our next step.

Bianca

Bianca, who is in her early sixties, came to see me after reading Michael Newton's books. She kept herself busy helping others, and was keen to make a difference in people's lives. Even so, she wondered if she was fulfilling her life's purpose. She had read about unconditional love and wanted to know how it felt to be loved unconditionally. She also hoped, during her life between lives session, that she would discover the lessons she was meant to learn in her current life. In total, Bianca had fifteen questions for the Council of Elders. I confidently told her that clients always had their questions answered.

On the way to the life between lives realm I always regress the client to a past life. As I guide Bianca back towards a past life, she encounters nothing but darkness. She seems stuck. We soon discover the reason for this difficulty.

Bianca is lying on the floor of a hut. The night is moonless and inside it is pitch black. She is holding her breath, and feels her heart beating against her ribcage.

Bianca is a married woman in her mid-twenties. She lives a simple life with her husband in a rudimentary village. The huts in this community are made mostly of bark and have earthen floors. The clothes they all wear are made of rough fabric in dull brown colours. They all work the fields. The weather is cool, probably autumn, and the place is England nearly a thousand years ago.

Bianca is lying up against a wall of the hut. In the darkness she starts feeling anxious.

I am waiting or listening for something. There are horsemen coming. Now they are here. They are riding through the village destroying everything. They are burning the huts and killing people with swords. I am trying to be small and hide in the dark. But they break into the house and cut me up. Slice me. I don't feel any pain.

It becomes apparent that Bianca does not know she has died. She is still hiding. She feels no pain because she has gone numb. I ask her if she needs to hide anymore.

She shakes her head.

I ask if hiding kept her safe.

No. The soldiers are determined. They want to clear out all the scum.

I hear a quiver in her voice. I ask if she still needs to hide from the soldiers.

No. Now I can look down and see. It is a bloody mess. Dirt and blood. I see my body. Going up further I see there are bodies everywhere. The soldiers are gone.

Life just goes so quickly. Luckily we have several lives.

Life isn't respected. It is such waste. A life cut short so quickly, so suddenly.

I am floating. There are clouds. Still floating. Just resting. I don't have to be afraid anymore. It is very nice. I am just floating in the clouds.

I ask if she wants to go home. Bianca starts crying quietly. 'Can I really go home?' she pleads. She needs ten minutes to recover. It seems she has felt lost for a long time.

She says she has moved upwards a little but once again she seems to be stuck.

I see a light but it is not clear. I am feeling quite peaceful but there is a block in my head. It needs to be removed. I can't function with it there. It is like a locked vault and I haven't got access to who I really am. It is all locked up.

Bianca complains that her head hurts as I gently probe to discover the nature of the block. It emerges that Bianca is disturbed because her life as the slaughtered peasant woman didn't seem to have any purpose. Her guides come in. Bianca describes them as 'a presence.' They help her gain a deeper understanding.

A life doesn't always have to have a purpose. I have to have certain experiences. The experience itself is enough. I don't always have to do stuff. It is enough just to be, to experience life without always striving. That life was important because it gave me the opportunity to experience humility. I have a tendency to want to do great things. I need to do ordinary things as well. It doesn't hurt to have a few messy deaths.

I need to learn to be patient. I always want to go some-

where. I am unique and it is enough just to be myself. I have read about this place [life between lives] *where people can go. So I have expectations that might not be met. I have to let go of what I have read and just allow my own journey to unfold.*

I have a feeling of excitement. An aliveness. There is something about appreciating that feeling. I don't have to do anything with it. It is a sense of being more alive. I just have to be it and radiate it. I am to relax and do whatever I feel like doing. I am supposed to enjoy my life.

All the bossy people in my life have an idea of how I should be, but I don't have to be what they expect.

I remind Bianca of her questions. Her guides give her more information.

The questions will be answered in good time. There is no point in talking about it. That is all in the head. Being in the head takes away the feeling. I need to focus my attention on my heart, body and feelings, rather than my thoughts and head.

I am asking where these needs came from—my need to prove myself by doing something worthy and my need to be approved of by significant others. 'Lighten up,' they said. 'Don't be so serious.' It is part of my soul nature to be serious and focused on doing things. It has been good and helped me develop but now it is getting in the way. If I want to expand I have to lighten up and realise that life is not that serious.

There is more to life than achieving. Being light and having fun is an important part of life. It is not supposed to be all work and no play.

I am being told that this is my life lesson. I am to appreciate life and lighten up. I need to let go of all expectations of others. No more mulling over things and judging. Instead, I need to be in a state of allowing. But most importantly, I am to live life with this feeling of aliveness. If I keep returning to this feeling and live it, then I am radiating unconditional love. Everything else is irrelevant. Nothing else is necessary.

I am surprised by these responses to her questions. I am used to having all my clients' questions answered, but I can see that asking the questions will pull her out of her feeling of aliveness, and back into thinking. I ask what we are to do with all her questions.

They [Bianca's guides] chuckle. Now is not the right time for questions. They don't want me back in my head. The most important thing for me right now is this feeling, this feeling of being connected and alive. All that other stuff is a distraction and I don't need to bother with it. It takes me out of really being in life and experiencing life.

I am being told to trust that the information will come when I need it. I always needed to know stuff and I would go searching for it. I collected information like a hoarder in case I needed it some day. I fill my head up with stuff I don't need. I don't need it until I need it and when I do need it, it will be there. It is about being present and not going off in my head thinking or worrying. It is as simple as that and as difficult as that.

Bianca spent another hour staying quietly connected to this powerful feeling that she described as 'aliveness'. In some traditions, such as Buddhism, this might be described as 'not doing'.

Her fifteen questions remained unanswered, although she was confident that she would receive answers at an appropriate time. Her purpose and her life lessons, however, were very clear. She knew exactly what she was to do. She was to connect to this sense of aliveness as often as possible.

George

George had been spiritually minded for the last twenty years. He was a gentle man and deeply distressed. In the last six months, he had been on an emotional roller coaster ride. He'd left an unhappy marriage of thirty years after finding the love of his life. With his beloved, he soared with feelings of joy and fulfilment. Then, when she went back to her abusive husband, he plummeted into despair and depression.

He'd thought he was destined to rescue his new love, Holly, from her unhappy marriage. Now that she was gone, he felt there was no purpose to his life. He was in his late fifties, well-off, and finished with his architectural career. Not long before he met Holly, he had taken up natural medicine. Until recently, he had loved it, but now it gave him no joy. Wherever he looked, he saw only emptiness. For the first time in his life, he found himself seriously considering suicide.

George had spent his life always doing what he thought was right. He was kind and thoughtful. Even the woman he left, his ex-wife, remained a friend. He couldn't understand why he now had to suffer so deeply.

He had felt so close to Holly, George thought they must share a soul connection. He deeply felt they were meant to be together. He wanted to know why the relationship hadn't worked out, and what he could do about it. He wondered if he had done something dreadful in a previous life. Could his present suffering be karmic punishment?

George did a past life regression and a life between lives regression. That meant we had the experience of two past lives and his present life to draw upon when making sense of his recent experiences. Both Holly and her husband made an appearance in both of those past lives.

In the first past life, they form a different relationship triangle. George's soul had incarnated as a young woman named Jane. Holly was Jane's mother, and Holly's present-day husband was Jane's stepfather.

I am wearing a dress that goes down to my ankles and clogs that are made out of wood. My hair is long and brown. I am happily shopping for bread in a village. It seems I routinely do the shopping as I am an only child. I am fifteen years old. The streets are cobblestone and the day is cool and cloudy. We live nearby. I am getting the feeling that something is going to happen. I don't like it. It is something disturbing.

I reassure Jane and suggest she be brave. She continues.

Someone grabs me. I have been dragged into a building, into a small room with stone walls. He rapes me. It is my stepfather.
He leaves and I go home. I have never liked him but I don't say anything. Why don't I say anything? [Jane cries deeply.] *Because my mother loves him!*

We progress to another scene in George's life as Jane.

It is nighttime. I am inside a cottage with a fire burning. I am thirty years old, living with my husband and our baby. Although I am contented I feel no passion for my husband. The rape has affected me. We argue. He wants sex and closeness and I don't. He is a good provider and he is caring. Still, I never told him about the rape. I never told anyone.

We move on to another scenario.

Now I am thirty-five and my mother is dying. I go to her. My stepfather is already dead. I decide to tell her about the rape. She doesn't believe me. She only thinks well of my stepfather, even though he was a hard man. I wonder why I bothered telling her. It didn't make any difference. I feel resigned.

Jane dies alone at age sixty. She feels only a sense of relief as she passes over.

George's guide tells him that his life as Jane was designed to learn about love. As Jane he was given the opportunity to express love unconditionally.

I didn't learn the lesson properly so I have to repeat [the experience]. *I am still struggling with unconditional love in my current life. Jane had resentment towards the man who raped her. Her inability to put it aside for her husband was not love. Neither was the lack of forgiveness for her mother for not believing her.*

My guide is telling me that to love unconditionally, I need to practice acceptance.

George faces the same challenge in the next regression he undertakes a few weeks later. This is his visit to his life between lives. Before reaching this realm, we regress to another past life.

Most often this is one's immediate past life. This was the case for George, whose past life occurred in the 1930s. He was called Vernon and he lived in a southwestern state of the USA.

Holly is my daughter. She is kneeling in front of me, crying. I have hit her. She is sixteen and she has been out with this boyfriend who I dislike. He is no good for her. He makes her unhappy because he is full of jealousy and anger.

It soon becomes apparent that this boyfriend is the same soul as Holly's husband in her current life.

Her mother has died many years ago and I brought her up alone. She and I are very close. There are no other children. I don't mind if she has boyfriends as long as they treat her well. She is pretty upset with me. She is heartbroken. She wants to be with this boyfriend and I won't let her.

We progress to another scene.

It is night and I am dying. I am in hospital after having had a heart attack. My daughter is beside me. She is in her early thirties and I am nearly sixty.

We are still close and she is visibly upset. She has been devoted to me. She is going to lose the only significant person in her life. She never married. She wasn't interested in the other boyfriends who came along because she was set on the first one. She gave him up because I demanded it.

I tell her I love her and I know she loves me. It is important that she has the chance to say goodbye. I seem to be at peace with dying.

George is quiet for a few minutes before I ask him what is happening.

It's quite bizarre. I'm finding it difficult to move on.

I spend about ten minutes helping him release his attachment to his daughter. I explain that hanging on doesn't help his daughter, who now needs to pursue her own life. He eventually lets go.

We move onto his life between lives. After being encased by a loving light that removes any leftover emotions, his guide appears. I ask about the purpose of his life as Vernon.

It is a bit of a rest point, nothing too challenging. For some reason, there was loneliness but also companionship. I was learning about having a love relationship in a non-sexual way. Mostly I succeeded. I probably shouldn't have interfered with my daughter's relationship with her boyfriend. Even though we parents might think we know what is best, we need to give our children the freedom to choose. That love was not quite unconditional.

George's guide suggests we go to a place that George describes as a meeting place, like a coffee shop. He recognises the other people there. It appears they will be involved in his current life as George.

We are in a coffee shop discussing the things we want to work on in our coming lives. It is all very broad at the moment. My eldest brother figures prominently in our plans with the group. He is going to help us resolve some karmic issues. He will take on the role of antagonist. We formulate our own rough plan, but it has to be approved by the Lords of Karma.

At the beginning of out session, George had described his eldest brother as the creator of copious grief for the family over the last twenty years. Apparently this brother tried to steal his mother's money and cost the family millions of dollars. None of the siblings speak to this brother.

It takes a hell of a lot of work to organise a lifetime. I cannot comprehend it. It is too complex.

Holly appearing in this life is only an option. I interfered with her plans in the past life and that needs to be adjusted in this coming life. It is tricky to get us to meet. We move in different age groups and circles. We decide to put it in the plan but we are not sure it will happen. Decisions will have to be made and free will, of course, can alter things.

I now explore the questions that George had composed for the life between lives session. These are all about his current life and his brief, intense relationship with Holly.

I am experiencing what I forced Holly to experience when I was her father. She had to shut down to the person she wanted to be with and now I have to shut down to being with her. There is some karmic thing between Holly and her husband. They have to work it out and it is important that they keep going until they do. They might get it sorted this lifetime. It is not that she doesn't want to be with me or that she doesn't love me; it is just that she has these other priorities. Being friends with me now is not possible. Her husband is the jealous type and staying friends would distract her. I succeeded in my role in her life by showing her what a loving relationship is like. That will help her with her purpose.

George was satisfied with the information he had received but he still had one major problem. How does he find fulfilment now Holly is gone from his life?

There is room to express unconditional love to some family members and I can focus on serving others. I can rest and enjoy life instead of it being so hard. Another relationship is possible. Even though I am scared, I could open up again. There are some areas where I could do further training. For example, there is a new natural therapy that interests me.

George did not receive what he had been hoping for in the sessions. He desperately wanted to be with Holly. He felt his life was empty without her. And he was seriously considering suicide if he could not be with her. If he knew, right at the beginning, that he would not get the assurances he craved, he might have baulked at undertaking the regression.

So he was surprised when he finally discovered that he and Holly were not meant to be together. Sure, he felt disappointed and sad, but he was no longer depressed and he was no longer suicidal.

The many hours George and I spent together were not therapy. We did not try to solve George's problems by talking about them. Instead, he actually relived the experiences that had led to his current situation. This time, as he explored his past lives, he saw them from a larger perspective. With this broad knowledge of his lives and his purpose, he could make sense of his current life and the deep grief he'd been suffering.

He understood why he'd felt such a strong bond with Holly. In one life he was her daughter; in the other she was his daughter.

He also discovered, in the first session, his major life purpose. His purpose was to learn to love unconditionally. He didn't manage to achieve this in his second past life but he was pleased to see that he had another chance in his current life.

George now knew exactly why his life and his relationships had followed a particular course. He also knew that he had to let Holly go.

Four years later I caught up with George. He hadn't seen Holly for years and was still friends with his ex-wife. He now had a successful healing business, using massage and other modalities. The testimonials on his website were glowing. No doubt he possessed a caring energy and a gift for healing. He was content with his life and found great satisfaction in helping people.

Amelia

Amelia came to her life between lives session hoping to experience her soul's wisdom and gain a better understanding of her life's purpose.

Amelia experienced a past-life in Northern Europe over a hundred years ago. She married the man she loved and had four children. Her life was much like the life of her mother and her grandmother before her. She baked, cooked, looked after the house, and cared for her carpenter husband and their children.

At the end of her life, her children and grandchildren are by her side. Her husband has already passed and she is looking forward to seeing him again. Her body is tired and her spirit is ready to go. She knows her family will be fine. She has cared for them lovingly and although they are sad to see her leave, she knows they will be sustained by the love she has bestowed on them.

She moves upwards and is met by her guides, one a male and one a female. She feels the different energies they emanate. The male has a strong, protective energy, while the female is softer and more caring. This combination restores her, and she feels a sense of wholeness, bliss and peace.

I feel like I am floating through an energy that is soft and velvet. It is strange because I have no body but I sort of feel like I do. I have the softest feathers all around me. Down, it is like goose down, caressing me, floating all around me while I am moving through it.

Amelia arrives in a garden. She explains that this is not a garden like those on Earth. There is no sun and yet there is light everywhere. All the trees, plants and flowers glow with a special light and there are more colors than she has ever seen before.

Amelia's guides sit with her in the garden while she reviews her past life. She discovers it was a rest life after a series of more challenging lives. The energies she took with her to Earth were mostly positive and they helped her achieve her purpose, which was all about love. She did well, as looking after and loving her family was a major part of her purpose for that past life.

Amelia wants to know about her current life's purpose. Her guides communicate to her through thoughts, telling her to be patient, as all will be revealed soon. First, they want to take her on a journey through the spirit world. This is also something that Amelia hoped to experience.

They fly off with her, and she arrives at the top of a high cliff with the ocean far below. Suddenly she sees colored energetic lights moving towards her. The lights are oval in shape and each one is a mix of different colors, like rainbows, but each one is unique in its combination of colors. As they come closer, she realises they are beings, or souls she has known for a long time. They surround her in a circle, drawing her into their beautiful light. It is her soul group and they are welcoming her back. She feels their loving light penetrating her in an exquisitely pleasant way.

Next, her guides take her to the library. Amelia can tell it is a library because it is filled with shelves of books. As she watches, the books start shimmering like holographs. It seems that they are alive. She receives the message that knowledge is energy and energy is knowledge, but not a solid, unchanging knowledge. The message is clearly given to her that knowledge has to be lived, not just accumulated and stored. She sees how the energies join, like a network of spider's webs, millions of them, all connected. They are all shimmering with energy.

She reaches out to touch one and a memory comes alive in her mind, and she sees the connection of this memory with other experiences she has had. She struggles to explain how profound this is for her, seeing the connections and the experiences resonating within her and influencing her future decisions. She can see how real wisdom comes from within, once one has reflected on many experiences and created the connections. She knows the information she needs at any time is available and can be accessed if she opens up to receive it.

She receives the message that trust is part of her purpose. She is to trust that any information that she needs will come. The time of studying is past. She needs to learn to trust her intuition.

Her guides now take her back to the cliff top. She recognises people from her current life, including her mother, her brother and some friends. She is told to look deeply into each one, one after another. As she looks closely at each individual, she automatically receives information about his or her strengths and weaknesses. She also understands how she can best interact with each of them to assist them on their soul journey. Amelia realises that these interactions are mutually beneficial—working with members of her soul family will aid her progress as she advances from life to life.

Now she is taken to a beautiful building of high columns and marble. She feels waves of energy flowing through her as she enters. It is like the power of this place is resonating out to all who come within its vicinity. The feeling is one of positive power, and the waves of energy are blends of blue and red, interacting together to form different hues of lilac and purple.

She realises she is to meet her Council of Elders. There are seven beings of light in front of her. The one in the middle is the spokesperson.

She energetically receives the message that she has done well. It comes to her as a feeling of loving energy that flows into her heart. It is so strong and beautiful that tears run down her cheeks.

She is told she is part of an important mission to help the energies change on the planet. She does this by blending together the Earth energies and the higher energies when she is in physical form.

She learns she has had many lifetimes. In some she was the perpetrator of violence, and others she was the victim. Many of her lives were very dark and she chose this path to progress quickly, so she could help the Earth changes. Her experience helps her energetically relate to others. She holds the positive energy for people who are struggling with the darkness inherent in the Earth system. By holding the positive energy she helps them lift their vibration to a point where sometimes they can feel lighter and loved.

The Council members tell her how much they value and support her work. Her purpose is to love people unconditionally. Some people love their false selves, and Amelia is told to accept them as they are. She realises these people are at a stage of development where this is the best they can do. Loving one's false self is better than not loving oneself at all.

The Council encourages her to continue her good work, and suggests she move onto another place of interest.

Amelia's guides take her to a place where other souls are working with energy. These spiritual beings are part of her work group and they are sending out streams of positive energies, like thought energy, to the humans and animals on Earth. This helps to raise the vibration of all beings on the planet and of the Earth itself. She understands that this is the work she does when she is in spirit. It is very similar to the work she is now doing while she is incarnated. This energy work is her specialisation, and her journey through all her many lives on Earth have brought her to this point where she is powerful enough to help others.

Amelia feels very satisfied with her journey through her life between lives and with the information she received about her purpose. She thanks her guides for their loving support and renews her determination to continue on her path and fulfill her purpose to benefit the Earth and all its inhabitants.

Danielle

Danielle, aged in her late thirties, knows what she wants from her session: 'To fit together the experiences I am having.' She hopes to understand the trust issues that have affected her relationships.

She experiences a past life as a female, named Alina, who lives in a community in a forest. Her skin is fair and her hair light brown. She wears pointed black leather shoes with a silver buckle. She notes that her shoes are dusty. The green dress she wears has puffed sleeves with a skirt that falls to the ground.

She sees people working in the forest clearing where they live. The men have beards and are chopping wood while the women are cooking. The huts are made from straw and sticks. It is Scandinavia, a long time ago.

We all work hard to survive. My parents live there and I am alone. I am having fun and I like helping the family. I am happy.

We move to another scene in Danielle's life as Alina.

I am outside and it is night. I am not feeling good. There are some mean people around. Very mean. They are trying to break up the whole community. They don't like us because we love nature. They don't understand us. We are peaceful people who love life. They don't like that. They are afraid.

They hit me. I beg them to stop. But they don't stop. They're hurting us... They are killing us and throwing us into graves.

Alina leaves her body and drifts upwards.

I can see the blue sky. Something is sparkling. I see sparkles everywhere. The sparkles are souls. They are around me now and I am moving upwards.

Now I see a shadow. It changes form. It is playing games with me. It is my guide making me feel comfortable.

I am not sure where I am now. I am resting.

We pause for a while as Danielle recovers from this life. Her guide gives her information about her life as Alina.

The men who came and killed us were naïve people. I am being told there is darkness as well as light. There are dark places and dark people. Lessons can be learnt from interacting with dark people.

These people who killed us will be shown their own lessons in time. That experience of killing will help them. They will have dark times in their lives and will learn compassion and understanding through these experiences.

They are cruel people. One is my grandfather in my current life. I am helping my grandfather.

I chose this life as Alina and I knew what would happen. I was okay with that. It was a useful life. I learned a lot. I learned that we are one with nature. We are one with all living things, good and bad. Even the cruel people, we are one with them too. I also learnt the benefits of being together in a community and learning to appreciate each other.

This life was a positive experience in spite of the violent end. My guide said I stood by what I believed in and never gave up. He is pleased and I feel peaceful.

Danielle is given more information about her life's purpose later from the Council of Elders.

The lives of Danielle and Alina are similar. My purpose, then and now, is to speak my truth. I am not to sacrifice what I know the truth to be by giving in and remaining silent against powerful people.

As Danielle, I have been the kind of person who wants to help by changing people. I cannot force change upon others. My purpose is to let them be and speak my own truth. Other people will watch and learn. If some don't like it, they are not ready.

My mother has a lot to learn. I am here to help her this lifetime. I need to say to her 'life is beautiful' and she will learn through my example of loving life.

I am to keep living my truth. When I feel connected to everything, animals and people, that is my truth. If I quieten my mind, I can connect. And I can do that all the time. It is about being loving and accepting but being honest as well.

My anxiety has come from the burden of disbelief. It will go if I just trust in life. The ego gives me false messages. A false message is dark, negative self-doubt. Let fears go.

I have no past issues to be concerned about. I am to just follow these instructions.

All the dark people play a role, not good or bad, it just is. Some people learn their lessons through pain. I don't need to have pain anymore if I just trust what happens and flow along with life freely.

If I think of the word release, I can access the feeling of peace and tranquility.

I am being told: 'You are to feel loved because you are loved.'

After the session, Danielle said, 'It was incredible…such a release. I felt it inside, outside, all around. It was truly an experience and more than I expected.'

Danielle's purpose reminded me of another case where the client was told that her purpose was to speak her truth. She was also encouraged to *live* her truth. The Council told her it is about saying *yes* when everyone else is saying *no*.

When I hear these words I see, in my mind's eye, a poster I have encountered with one fish, a little different to the others, swimming in the opposite direction.

This message, of speaking and living our truth in the face of opposition from others, is one that is frequently given to people in their life between lives. Of course, before we can live our truth we have to know what that is. As Danielle's Council mentioned, the ego and our fears can hijack us and throw us off-track.

Conclusion

From the cases outlined here, it seems we plan our lives and set goals that we hope to achieve. Although this is generally true of the people who come to visit their life between lives, it does not mean everyone on the planet plans their life.

I have heard some spiritual gurus suggest that souls are all different and at different stages of awareness. Some souls might plan their next incarnation in detail, some might do no planning at all, and others lie somewhere in between these two extremes. The analogy of high school graduates illustrates the point. Some graduates know what they want to do from a young age and plan the steps needed to fulfil their goals. Some plan loosely. Others do no planning at all and wait for opportunities to arise.

However it works, many people sense they do have a purpose, especially people who decide to undertake a spiritual regression. And I have noticed that people with no sense of purpose usually feel lost.

People who visit their life between lives find the experience greatly rewarding. One major satisfaction is gaining clarification on the nature of their life's purpose.

The BIG Picture

The only limits to personal insight are self-imposed.

MICHAEL NEWTON

Most people decide to do a regression to gather more information about personal challenges in their lives. But not everyone is focused purely on personal issues. Some people want answers to the big questions in life. They want to know the nature of reality and why humanity is the way it is. A life between lives session is the perfect place to receive these answers.

During your session, you have access to a panel of wise beings. Collectively, these beings are known as the Council of Elders. The Council answers your questions in creative ways so you will receive the understanding you seek.

Before the session, the client writes down a list of questions that he or she wants answered. The client receives the answers from the Council or their guides, and tells me so I can record them. In effect, the questioner is the client and the responder is the Council. Even though some clients doubt that their questions will be answered, these doubts are unfounded. The answers will always be given, nearly always during the session. If they are not given during the session, they will come to the client soon after.

In this chapter, we explore some of the answers that have been given to the big questions clients have asked. Of course, these answers will have been tailored to the personality and needs of the questioner. However, useful information about the purpose of our lives on Earth and how the system works can be gleaned from these important interactions.

Ben

In the following dialogue, I ask the questions that Ben has prepared, while Ben channels the Council's answers. Because Ben wanted to know more about the big picture, I also ask probing questions on his behalf.

The Council of Elders gave Ben the answers he sought, often accompanied with images. The Council said he had incarnated on Earth a thousand times, and that he was three-quarters of the way there.

BEN: What is 'there'?

COUNCIL: Union with the creator.

BEN: But didn't we start there? Why do we leave, only to come back?

COUNCIL: It is like putting metal in the fire to make it stronger.

BEN: Why does it need to be stronger?

COUNCIL: It is about the ever-expanding universe.

BEN: Is the universe always expanding?

COUNCIL: Yes.

BEN: What is our role in that?

COUNCIL: The universe cannot expand without what you humans provide.

BEN: Can they help us to understand what we are providing?

COUNCIL: It is energy.

The Council responded with silence

BEN: What sort of energy?

COUNCIL: Stronger energy. More expansive. Increased creation.

BEN: What is creation?

COUNCIL: Expanding the universe.

BEN: Can you elaborate?

COUNCIL: It is about your thoughts, your actions and your experiences. You do things that surprise us. Humans can do new and amazing things, and that is creation.

BEN: Is it just going to expand forever?

COUNCIL: Probably.

BEN: Why is expansion important?

COUNCIL: If you don't expand, you contract.

BEN: How did it all begin?

The Council responded with silence. Ben then reported that he was being given an image of a heart with a spider-web around it. I asked the Council to explain the image.

COUNCIL: It's a big circle. A new soul comes out of the nursery. It experiences life. It finishes reincarnating and then goes back to the original energy source stronger. That keeps the expansion going. Humans are all of that.

BEN: In what way are we stronger?

COUNCIL: It is about knowledge but more than knowledge. It is seeing the interconnectedness of everything. The spider-web represents interconnectedness.

Ben then reported seeing a massive, three-dimensional web.

COUNCIL: Getting stronger is about your awareness of the interconnectedness. You need to see how an action or thought impacts on the other parts. It is learning how things relate to each other. And this awareness needs to be constant. You need to think before you take any action.

BEN: How do you create with the energy?

COUNCIL: You make your light bigger and you do that with your mind. You think about what you want to create with a lot of intent. Then you can make your creation manifest. You can shape things by intentional thought.

BEN: Is God perfect? Why has this 'perfect' God made all these imperfect people?

COUNCIL: It is not about perfection. It is about expansion.

BEN: Where do the guides fit in? Do we become guides?

COUNCIL: The guides help you all to keep expanding. Souls who have incarnated can become guides.

BEN: What about angels? Are they real or are they just other souls?

COUNCIL: They are souls.

BEN: Have they incarnated?

COUNCIL: They are not in between incarnations.

BEN: Angels haven't incarnated?

COUNCIL: Incarnation is not their job. They are angels. They come to help you. Their energy is white and fresh. They are just different.

BEN: Are they loving?

COUNCIL: They are different to what you know as loving. Protective is a better description. When you hear stories of someone narrowly avoiding a tragedy, then the angels have been involved. Or if you were saved from a situation and then the person who saved you disappears. That was an angel. This happens when you get yourself into something that is not in your plan or you went further than you should have. The angels look after you.

BEN: What are Creators?

COUNCIL: When you have finished incarnating, you can become a Creator.

BEN: Do you mean a Creator of universes?

COUNCIL: When you are finished incarnating you can create your own universe, but it has to fit in with the overall plan.

BEN: Who is the overall planner?

COUNCIL: The energy.

BEN: Is our physical world a virtual reality?

COUNCIL: Yes.

Ben said he was given a vision of millions of lights, suns and planets, and there were spider-webs connecting them all.

After Ben came out of the trance, he said the experience of receiving the information could not be fully portrayed in words. He received visions and a deep sense of what the Council meant. He was very satisfied with the wisdom he was given. He said he retained a deep understanding of what our soul journeys are all about.

Lily

Lily was interested in the plans or contracts we make, at the soul level, before we reincarnate. In her session, she had experienced a past life where she felt she had died prematurely. She was upset because she had not finished her life's work, and that work had been benefiting many people.

Other Lives, Other Realms

The Council explained that her early death was part of the contract she made before she incarnated. There were good reasons for the early death. The good work she was doing expanded as a consequence of her death. The Council continued:

There can be disagreements between the individual soul and the physical person. The contract is made by the soul. Your physical self might not agree with the contract as you play it out. You, as a human, can get very involved on the earthly plane, too involved. You can get very serious about what you are doing on Earth. You forget that life is just a game. You don't really die.

Lily also wanted to know what options in her life she should pursue and what she should avoid. The Council pointed out that some souls reach a level of development where they can relax and trust. Lily was now at that level. They continued:

At this stage in your development you do not need to take on anything that does not give you joy. Pushing yourself to take on various tasks and overcome obstacles has been important in the past. That was when you were a younger soul. Now you need to trust the opportunities that come to you rather than seeking out specific opportunities. Don't make things happen. If it is meant to happen, it will happen. Don't knock on doors that are not easily opened. You can be proactive once the opportunity is there.

To release any feelings of constriction, flow more with the good opportunities that come your way. These will be obvious to you, especially when you are rested, relaxed, open and trust-

ing. Then you are in a more expanded state and can see where to go. Duty is the danger. Don't act out of duty. Act from the heart.

Lily wanted to know how she could make her life more joyful. The Council pointed out the importance of letting go of the past. They continued:

Instead of looking for explanations about the past and what you did not understand, you can override the past by realising that all experiences are subjective anyway. Everyone does 'good' things and everyone does 'bad' things. Everyone makes mistakes, learns and changes course. How you judge yourself is all just a perspective.

When you really, really get it, you know it is all just a game. Then you can change anything in the past. The past doesn't influence you anymore. At the end of the day, the past is nothing more than multiple points of view. Nothing is concrete. You can change it.

Looking at something differently rewrites it for you. It changes history. When you change your perspective, everything changes. It was as real as it could be in the moment when it happened. But now it is in the past and just a memory. There are many ways of looking at that experience that is now just a memory.

Culture is an accumulation of memories and beliefs. Culture is nothing real. You take on the beliefs of those around you, until you let them go. It is important to initiate change. When you help others you help them change perspective. Change is useful. Remember, nothing is concrete. Everything can be changed. You can rewrite and change it all at any point. You don't need to be constrained or limited by past experiences.

Lily had more questions for the Council. Again, I asked on Lily's behalf, while she channelled the Council's answers.

LILY: What forms each life?

COUNCIL: Choice. You choose it all.

LILY: Who is the 'you' that does the choosing?

COUNCIL: The soul with many experiences.

LILY: Do we have many lives to gain these experiences?

COUNCIL: Some souls learn fast, some souls learn slowly. It is about the quality of the experience, not the quantity.

LILY: How do we choose our Earth life?

COUNCIL: We help you. After you make your choices, you live them. It is like painting a picture or choosing an avatar in a computer game. You are locked into the choices you made but you are not locked into how you play it.

LILY: Do you help us?

COUNCIL: When you know how to access our support, you can ask for help. You draw what you desire into you. Ask and it will be given.

LILY: Where does this come from?

COUNCIL: You can draw it from anywhere. You draw the energy you need from the greater wisdom.

LILY: If I wanted to be a great musician, could I draw musical ability from a great musician who has passed over?

COUNCIL: Yes. Then you practice your instrument and use the inspiration that comes to you. How you express yourself through that instrument is the key. You learn about expression.

Learning to play music is a tool. It is not important in itself. What is important is the opportunity to express your uniqueness through the music.

LILY: Why do we keep coming back, life after life?

COUNCIL: You ask to come back.

LILY: Has my guide lived on the planet?

COUNCIL: No.

LILY: Is he a part of my soul?

COUNCIL: No.

LILY: What is the role of a guide and how does that system work?

COUNCIL: Your guide is part of a different drama, a different game. He is playing a game too, the game of being a guide.

LILY: What is time?

COUNCIL: There is no such thing. There is only the moment. The idea of time is just a perspective.

LILY: Do we have soul groups?

COUNCIL: People like school trips. They like to experience things together. The people who are with you in a life are part of the choices you made when you planned your life. You decide with whom you incarnate.

David

During his life between lives session, David received some general information about the purpose of our lives and what is needed to transcend the cycle of Earth incarnations. You have met David before in two earlier chapters. In the first he experienced a past life as a monk. In the second, he saw the patterns of behavior that unfolded over many lifetimes. Here, David is taken to the library and given a book. This book is about all of his past lives.

*My guide and I are walking around, watching people study-
ing in a library. I see there are rows and rows of books.*

*He feels that I have gone backwards somewhat. He wants
to show me some of things I have done. I might be here to
study for a while before going back to earth.*

Interestingly, David spent two hundred years between his last
incarnation in the early eighteenth century and his present life.
In this current era, when there is so much opportunity to reincarnate, most souls have a much shorter time between lives, often
no more than a decade.

It is good to be back here but I feel a bit disappointed.

*We have found the librarian and she is finding my book.
My book is now on the table and I am looking at the first page.*

*It is like a regular book but with holographic pop-ups. As
a kid I had those pop-up books but these pop-ups are alive, like
watching a 3D movie.*

*I am told when I started off in physical form I showed
great promise.*

*I am looking at a battle scene. I am a Roman Centurion
and we are victorious. I was instrumental in winning these
battles.*

Now we are turning to the next page. It's another life.

*More battles, but now I am on the other side. On the left
page I am fighting in Northern Europe, near Saxony, against
the Romans. It is very bloody. On the right page I am in another life, fighting in North Africa. I see elephants. This time,
I'm a Roman soldier again.*

I see a horrible irony. In one life I fight for one side. Then we die and meet the same foes in the next life. But now you and your old foes have changed sides.

It doesn't matter who or what you fight for. It is all about the role you take and the way you play with what you are given. That is what determines your true character. It is about how the character perseveres.

As I turn the pages, I see different people and different lives. I am still involved in a military role but now I'm becoming a spy. I died a lot in those early lives by being caught. I got better at spying and I learned to read people.

Then I made a change. I became more of a recluse and lived a more peaceful life. I became more spiritual. I wanted to pay my karmic debts. In the roles I had played as a spy, I betrayed people and I felt a need for atonement.

There are pages and pages of me being in conclaves. I helped people in various lives and various places. Not all of them were in the church.

As I age in each of those roles, I become more influential and I am able to help people. Predominately, I had lives in religious orders but in many different traditions. Often I am born into religious families.

There were a lot of inspiring people in those lives. I became caught up in the idea of transcending the physical and breaking the cycle of incarnation. I wanted to free myself from the physical realm.

My guide is telling me that I can try to shortcut it all if I want but I won't get the true understanding without the full experience of Earth. One has to undergo the complete journey to fully understand the Earth experience.

He says the experience of many human lives gives us the understanding that allows transcendence. We have to get the lessons from the human lives in the first place, in order to learn how to transcend the physical. There is no point sending you back if you are not going to take advantage of that full experience of Earth.

He also says it's harder to break patterns of behavior if you do the same thing lifetime after lifetime, such as being a spiritual devotee. You do not progress in your learning if you keep taking the same path.

David lived many lives as a Buddhist monk, trying to achieve enlightenment. He was told that this quest is futile until he has experienced and understood the complete nature of physical life.

In some regressions, people just get a snippet or two of information that is useful. I have decided to share some of these insights with you.

Matt

Matt experiences a past life on twelve tropical islands where there is great abundance, love and peace. The inhabitants celebrate their lives, feeling great gratitude for all they have and love for one another. In the past life, Matthew dies and meets with a number of light beings.

The guides are saying this past life is to show that the universe will provide. There is no lack. Love is real. Everything else is illusion.

This experience of abundance is for the future children

to bring light to the darkness in the world. Light travels to darkness, the darkness doesn't travel to the light.

The children of those islands bring light to the world. They are now masters, twelve masters from the twelve islands. They fell and came to earth. They came to understand what Earth was like from the human perspective and they did get caught up in the ego experience. They used to fight with each other but they stopped and saw the truth. They came back to knowing that love is the only reality. Everything else is an illusion. This is the message for the world.

Now there is a shift in Matthew. Instead of reporting what he receives, these light beings now speak through him, introducing themselves by saying: 'We are Twelve. We are One.'

I ask them questions about the past life, who they are and if they have any more messages for us.

Everyone is the message. The message whispers. You don't find your purpose, you live it. You are finding your true self, finding love.

You can flow. Your fear, desperation and anxieties are against the flow. Suffering comes from resisting the flow.

You all have the same destination. If you go with the flow, the journey is happy. You don't need all this suffering. Fear is what brings suffering, the fear of letting go of control. Control itself is an illusion. It comes from your ego. There are no mistakes. You can relinquish control and go with the flow. You will all arrive at your destination.

All the suffering is an illusion, just resistance.

At the time of receiving this message, I didn't fully understand what these high-level beings mean by flow. Now I know that flow means to trust and allow, instead of worrying and fighting whatever is happening. You are in the flow when you know absolutely there are no mistakes, that you are ultimately taken care of and everything that is happening is meant to be happening. There is a larger plan. We humans are not in control and do not need to be.

Andrew[1]

During Andrew's life between lives session, he met the Council of Elders. They looked like judges and wore wigs and rich, red robes.

Andrew was worried because of bad things he had done in his past life as a soldier in the First World War. He thought he might go to hell.

Andrew quickly became aware that he had already judged himself, and the Elders were only playing along with his expectations. Soon their wigs and robes were gone and they were sitting around on leather lounge chairs chatting with him as a colleague. Andrew described this as sharing information.

Andrew mentioned that the Council knew the war was coming decades before it was declared.

Andrew discovered that the personality of a human is made up of many intentions, including the intention of the Council, the parents, the soul itself and many other influences. The soul may not be the prime mover because it might not know enough about its needs. A human is like the project undertaken by a design and implementation team.

---

1 You will meet Andrew again in the chapter, *Redemption.*

Some of the life is planned and much remains simply as possibilities. Possibilities are pruned away by choices as one is drawn in a particular direction.

Any individual can tap into the consciousness of any other person who has lived, if his or her desire is strong enough. Of course, one still has to learn the necessary skills. For example, if you wish to be a pianist, your body and brain need to learn to work together, so you can play the piano well. Then you can access inspiration from any of the great pianists of the past.

The Council said there are many opportunities in this era for people to access the information they need. They can choose to be open or they can choose to be closed. People who choose to be closed can be brutal. There is brutality on Earth and that is available as a choice. Currently Earth life offers a smorgasbord of opportunity.

People can talk themselves up but underneath they are haunted by the shame they have accumulated. They have no balance. More information is not the solution. They need to take the longer view, the expanded view. The roots we have are much deeper than a single entity born in this era.

Morris

Morris, who you met earlier, received some advice from his guide after experiencing a life as a soldier in the Second World War, when he had to kill the enemy.

I am being asked how I felt about killing people during the war. I tell my guide I had to do it, but I didn't like it.

My guide is asking me to compare how that is different to a previous life where I killed out of my own free will.

I felt it was necessary for the greater good in the life of Walter [the soldier], *even though I didn't enjoy it.*

She [Morris's guide] *is telling me not to be hard on myself for killing the enemy. It was for the greater good. She is telling me that there is a lot of human evolution that needs to take place before we have a true choice. She means that humans have a long way to go before we reach the point where we can refuse to kill.*

Everyone will have to be at peace before we have free will about killing.

Morris was also given some general advice from the Council about how free will interacts with predetermination.

You plan your lives. For the greater part, you all choose the events you will experience in your lives, although not every eventuality can be predetermined. If you are not involved in the events you need to experience, you will leave the physical realm. You leave when there is no growth or forward movement.

There are other things that can happen apart from your main learning. These may be useful or they may be detrimental. You will just come across them. Sometimes it is the free will of others playing out. Sometimes it is your free will in action.

You choose your life and the probabilities. It is correct that this choice is at a general level. Within that choice there is some room to move when you are physical.

Peter

During his life between lives session, Peter asked if it is possible to be free while living in a human body. The Council replied:

In a sense, yes. Being tied to a body is difficult for a soul. Go flying to get a sense of what a soul feels like when it is free from a body. Love will set you free. And laughing is good for the soul too.

Many people who experience a life between lives session gain a sense of being without a body. People who have a near death experience feel this too. They often comment on the discomfort of returning to the body. Clients also comment on how heavy they feel after coming out of the trance, having experienced the lightness of being in the higher realms.

The advice from the Council reminds me of my friends who love flying in light aircraft. They report feeling a sense of freedom when they are in the sky. Even more so if doing aerobatics, where they toss the plane around in seemingly boundless space.

Timing

It seems the timing for a regression is important. Many Newton Institute practitioners discover that when appointments are delayed for some practical reason, the changes in timing are meant to be. During the sessions, we have been told that certain energies need to be in place to achieve the outcomes our clients desire.

I do not know a lot about astrology, but I suspect the placement of the planets plays a key role in ensuring the energies are appropriate.

I always trust the timing will be right. If the client requests a time but that is not available, I expect we will find another that is right for the regression.

Dimensional Transgression

I have had two clients who said they survived incidents that should have been fatal. Both occurred while driving. One miraculously 'flew over' a semi-trailer that had broken down, completely blocking the road. The other blinked as he was driving fast towards the edge of a cliff, only to find he was inexplicably back on the road, continuing forward. Both incidents were witnessed by passengers. The first client asked about it during his session.

He was told this sudden, impossible-seeming shift is called a 'dimensional transgression', and it happened to remind him of his divinity. Nothing happens by mistake, they said. All is for the higher good.

Earth Changes

Many clients are told they are here to help bring about vibrational changes that are taking place on the planet. The high-level intelligent beings tell us that the Earth energies need to balance. Further inquiries reveal that light needs to balance dark. There will always be dark and there will always be light, and the two need to be in equilibrium.

We are told that the new era—referred to as the Earth Changes—also involves balancing male and female energies.

The end of 2012 ushered in a shift, which is a major change

for humans. Over the last two thousand years, humans have been greatly influenced by strong masculine energies. As more of the feminine energies come in, people will find it easier to express loving and nurturing thoughts and actions. This will take time but will ultimately help heal the planet.

The people who bring about most change in our lives are not usually high profile, such as those who preach, make the news, or achieve fame. The people who work quietly in the background bring about the most change in our world, particularly positive energetic change.

Conclusion

When you undertake a life between lives regression, you are given the opportunity to ask many questions. All our clients, save one, have received answers to their questions. In that instance, the client was in a blissful place, and the Council wanted her to integrate those feelings. They said she spent too much time in her head, seeking intellectual answers. They reassured her that the answers will come to her when she most needs them, most likely while she is meditating.

The answers we receive during a life between lives session are not limited to words. Rather, the answers come alive in us. They become part of our lived experience. Clients have to translate this experience into words so it can be recorded for them to access later.

By the time I come to ask my clients' prepared questions, many have already been answered. The past life, meeting with the guide, and visiting the library or life selection area will have provided much of the information sought.

When it comes to the big picture, the individual is sometimes given other-worldly experiences. For example, one person was drawn into a light that became an enormous cherishing flower. She had tears running down her face as she absorbed so much love she wondered if her circuits would explode.

The answers are always provided to the person who asks. Therefore, they reflect the culture, the beliefs and level of development of each person. Nevertheless, some of the information outlined in this chapter may resonate with you personally. I suggest you take those ideas on board, and leave behind anything that jars.

Body Selection

You don't have *a soul. You* are *a soul. You* have *a body, temporarily.*
WALTER M. MILLER JR., SCIENCE FICTION WRITER

You might find it hard to believe, but we select our bodies before we are born! Mind you, this choice is not completely ours. It's actually the responsibility of our soul-selves—which can lead to problems if we're not happy with our soul's choice. Remember, we are much more than just our physical bodies and human personalities. Sometimes our human personality may find itself at odds with our soul's intentions. This can affect our self-esteem and enjoyment of our physical life.

If you are dissatisfied with your physical body, understanding why your soul chose it on your behalf can be greatly freeing. Our souls have a higher calling—to ensure our ongoing spiritual evolution—so there are always sound reasons behind the choices they make. Life is much easier when we accept our bodies, regardless of their flaws.

Most people visiting their life between lives do not encounter the body-selection area. However, those who are guided to this unique realm find it a most enlightening experience. The following cases illustrate this point.

In the first example, Morris asked the Council of Elders a question about his body. The Elders suggested that he would find his answer in the body-selection area.

163

In the second case, Nadia's guide took her to the body-selection area. Until then she had no idea that such an area existed. Nadia had always hated her body and suffered from a poor self-image. Her visit to the body-selection area was no accident. Her disgust with her body was about to be seriously challenged.

In the last case, Crystal wanted to know why she had chosen her very large, short body. Both her guides accompanied her to the body selection area in her life between lives.

Morris

Although Morris was only in his thirties, he had already had a bout of cancer. He was in remission after being treated with chemotherapy. You might remember Morris from the chapter on *Healing*, where he received advice on how to deal with his illness.

During the session, Morris joins with his soul-self. Together, they ask the Council of Elders why his body is weak and prone to illness. He is directed to the body-selection area.

Once there, Morris notices a large screen. His guide asks him to sit in front of the screen, explaining that Morris will be shown the four possible bodies that he was offered before embarking on his present life. Accepting one of the bodies also means accepting a range of other circumstances—nationality, family of origin, talents and interests, and, of course, gender.

The first person he sees is a dark-skinned male of African ancestry. This man looks tall, broad, strong and robust. He will be born in Germany and adopted by white German parents. In addition to the challenges posed by his adoption, he will also be bullied when he goes to school. Because of his strength, he could overcome the challenge of being bullied. Due to his natural physical prowess, he is likely to become passionate about sport and find solace in his sporting abilities.

Next, Morris sees on the screen a white Caucasian male who will be born in Denmark. This man has a smaller body than the African. He will be very bright and intellectual and his family is very stable. Events will flow smoothly for most of his life. He will eventually face challenges, but these will come much later on.

Now there appears a Caucasian female who would be born in Greece. She is tall with thick, dark hair and a very beautiful face and body. Her father will pass away before she is born and the lack of this bond in her early life will greatly affect her. She will actively pursue intimacy while also fearing it. This will cause her to have many male and female relationships.

Finally, Morris sees a white English male. This man is small and slight. His parents will divorce early and he will not have a good relationship with his stepfather. This body is very sensitive and carries a high potential for illness. Morris sees that this would be a tough life.

Morris pauses, and reflects on the purpose of his life. He wants to create experiences that will enable him to realise his true power. His true power involves more than his physical body and more than his physical will. His true power is intuitive. It requires him to connect with his soul-self and allow this higher energy to shine through him. Once he has achieved a strong connection with his true power, he wants to use this loving light and wisdom to help others come into their true power.

Our lives are about learning and some souls like to proceed quickly in the classroom of Earth life. Morris is one of these souls. He does not choose easy lives. To accomplish his ambitions in this coming life, he needs a body and background that will provide significant challenges.

Morris now evaluates his different choices.

The African faces two significant challenges: being adopted by a white family, and later being bullied at school. However, with such a large powerful body, he might use his physicality to get through. For example, he might be tempted to stand up to people and intimidate them, rather than developing his compassion and wisdom. If he relied on his superior physical strength, he might never awaken to the fact that he is more than his physical body. This would mean that his intuitive abilities would be neither realised nor utilised.

Morris decides that the Danish life would not serve him, either. Being born into a stable family would allow him to easily succeed in the world. The opportunity to develop his intuitive abilities would not appear until late in his life. Morris does not want to waste time. He would prefer to meet some significant challenges earlier in life, and then move quickly towards his goals.

The Greek woman is too pretty. Lacking a strong male role model in her life, she will hide behind her beauty, hoping it will shield her from life's harsher lessons. As a result, she is destined to have many superficial relationships. Morris believes he will be better able to develop his intuitive abilities if he can forge a strong, steady relationship.

Morris chooses the slight English male, believing that a frail body and a fractured family will help him achieve his goals. His guide insists that it will be a very hard life. She asks him if he understands all the implications of this choice.

Morris reassures her that he is pleased with his choice, because he wants to learn quickly. Being sensitive to illness creates risks; it also presents Morris with opportunities to transcend his physical body. His sensitivity offers another advantage: it makes him more open to connecting with his higher soul-self.

Morris wants to know his true power. True power is not physical. True power is a pure, positive energy that comes from above. Whenever we open to that pure, positive connection, it flows through us. Morris can see that by having a weaker body, he will be driven to find non-physical sources of power. Being gifted with a strong intellect, like the Danish man, might jeopardise his chances of connecting with his higher self. Such higher-level connection comes through our intuition, not our intellect. The physical strength of the African and the physical beauty of the Greek also pose problems. Strength and beauty can focus one's attention on the physical rather than the spiritual. The weaker, non-intellectual body of the Englishman is perfect for his purposes. Morris is happy with his choice.

After the session, Morris said he was now happy with his sensitive body. He understood why he made that choice. He could also see why he had struggled with illness and other challenges. He was keen to use his creative powers to heal his body.

Nadia

At a critical moment during the session with Nadia, I ask her where we should go next. We are immediately taken to the body-selection area. Nadia has never read any books by Michael Newton, so she has no idea that there is such a place. She describes what she sees.

I am in a room that looks like a fashion store. But there are no clothes. Instead there are body suits. I don't like it here. It is grotesque. I don't want to be here.

Nadia's guide stands beside her. He is trying to tell her something, but she cannot hear it. I know that this means she is not open to the information. It clashes with her beliefs and, even though she thinks she wants to hear it, there is a stronger part of her that refuses to listen.

Earlier, while she was visiting the Council of Elders, the Council gave her the gift of courage. I remind her of this gift, as well as her desire to know the truth. I ask her to open to the information her guide is presenting, even though she may find it challenging.

She listens for a minute or two, then suddenly exclaims, 'He said I chose every piece of my body! Why the hell would I do that?'

Nadia has never liked her body and it makes no sense to her. Sadly, disliking our bodies disconnects us from our soul-selves because we focus so strongly on our physicality, and the limitations it imposes. Being disconnected, Nadia does not want to take responsibility for selecting a body that she rejects.

This idea stops Nadia in her tracks. She is reluctant to move forward. I talk about her desire to know the truth and give her an exercise that will increase her courage. Nadia loves horses, so I ask her to imagine riding a powerful white stallion at full gallop.

About half a minute later, Nadia says, 'I am ready.'

I ask her where she is now.

Nadia replies, 'We are in the belly section.'

Again, Nadia tenses up. The belly section makes her nervous.

She does not want to look that way. I gently challenge her. Reluctantly, she agrees to keep going.

Gradually, Nadia starts receiving information. She says she chose the 'Belly of Abandonment' for her life as Nadia. She doesn't know why she chose it and she doesn't know why it is called the 'Belly of Abandonment.' Her natural curiosity kicks in, and she soon discovers that her paternal grandmother had the same type of belly. This grandmother was abandoned several times in her early life. Her biological mother abandoned her when she was a baby. Her adoptive family then abandoned her when she was a child. The father of her first child abandoned her when she was a young adult. This man went back to his wife in France and left Nadia's grandmother to fend for herself in China. The child, who was abandoned along with his mother in China, grew up and fathered a daughter. This daughter is Nadia.

At a soul level, Nadia deliberately chose this belly and its emotional burdens. She describes the belly as protective. It grows bigger as one overeats. This overeating is triggered by feelings of abandonment. The emotional eating provides comfort and the large belly feels comfortable too. Nadia discovers that her father and brother have also chosen this belly. The guide explains why.

The emotional energy of abandonment has come down the ancestral line. Your grandmother succumbed to the influence of this energy. Having given in to her deep feelings of abandonment, she increased the hold this energy held over her, and over her descendants. This energy still prevails in the ancestral line and needs to be cleared. By choosing this belly, you hoped to release the pattern of abandonment that had afflicted your family for generations.

She is told how she might achieve this release. Her guide suggests she research and write her grandmother's story. The emotional energy trapped in her maternal line can only be released physically. Writing out the grandmother's story will enable Nadia to connect fully with the grief of abandonment. Once she connects with this grief, she will be given the opportunity to fully understand its nature, to grieve the pain it has caused, and let it go. This will not be an intellectual process. Nadia will be racked with pain. She will weep; she will cry out. While agonising, this experience is necessary if she is to transcend the deep sense of loss that the Belly of Abandonment has caused her ancestral line.

Nadia's grandmother died of lung cancer, and Nadia is told that this will be her fate too if she cannot release this burden and break the pattern.

I ask Nadia's guide if there is more to know here in the body-selection area, or if we should move on. I am told there is much more to do here.

The guide tells Nadia that while she chose her mother's nose, other features such as her eyes and chin come from her father. Nadia is quite happy with this. Now we head off to the reproductive section.

'This is really weird,' Nadia says, 'Gee, you wouldn't believe what comes in many different sizes… Oh, I've just been told that I chose the Womb of Wonder.'

'The Womb of Wonder?' I ask. 'Why is it called the Womb of Wonder?'

'Because you wonder why it doesn't work properly!' Nadia exclaims. We both chuckle.

Nadia discovers that she also chose the narrow hips that went along with this womb. She wasn't the only one in her family that made this choice. Her maternal grandmother chose it and Nadia feels that other female ancestors did too.

The guide explains why all these women chose the same combination.

These women are afraid they will not be good mothers, and yet the children have to be born. Their births are pre-destined. The inadequate womb and narrow hips lead to the mother's death in childbirth. Nadia's grandmother died in childbirth, while Nadia was saved by modern medicine. This womb and the psychological torment it represents are further burdens that Nadia is being called upon to release from the family line.

Nadia has two children. By surviving childbirth and building her confidence in her mothering skills, she is gradually releasing this pattern. Sometime after the session, Nadia's son investigates that particular ancestral line and discovers that seven women died in childbirth.

Although Nadia expressed great reluctance when she first ventured into the body-selection area, she is pleased she made the trip there. She feels much more at peace with her body and is happier in herself. Just as we are about to leave this area, Nadia exclaims, 'Isn't this an amazing place!'

Five years later, I catch up with Nadia. A few months after the session, she participated in a supportive writing retreat in France where she began outlining the story. She has thought about the book many times since but became caught up in her business. Nadia is only fifty so she has plenty of time to write her grandmother's story, which remains her intention.

Crystal

Crystal is short, sweet and obese. She has been to see me many times and she has experienced several past life regressions. She has faced a lot of disturbing lives with various challenging experiences. In fact, her guides told her she is living four lives in one. This was explained to mean she has taken on four times as many challenges as most souls take on in one life.

Crystal wants to know why she chose her body. Her guides, Abu and Aslan, are present. Abu leads her to the place when she can learn about this choice. Here is the dialogue that followed.

CRYSTAL: I see a big, big white palace with domes and minarets. I am in this really, really big room. Sounds horrible but we are in a butcher's cold room. Bodies are hanging—not on hooks, but on hangers. So weird. I think I must be crazy. There are no heads on these bodies. They look like costumes. They hang like clothes hanging on racks in a store. The racks are grouped in circles so you can walk around and look at different bodies. It is bizarre. The room is huge and there is a long table in middle of this vast, elongated space. The guides put some bodies on the table so I can look at them. The bodies are complete except there are no heads.

KAREN: How did you choose your body?

Crystal begins to weep.

KAREN: Do you know why you are crying?

CRYSTAL: I want to choose it and I don't want to choose it. It seems really stupid. To carry everything I need to carry in this life, I need to choose a big body. *[Crystal is still crying.]*

KAREN: Is there anything specific we can know about choosing this big body?

CRYSTAL: I don't know what this has got to do with it but I am now in a room with Aslan and it is so beautiful. The whole room, the walls, the drapes, everything is beautifully reflective like the icebergs, like the white and aqua blue of icebergs. Aslan is writing multiplication tables on a board. The board is the same aqua. He is writing on the board in lilac and the script appears like velvet. The thick marker he is using is gold, real gold, and all is ornately engraved. There is no floor. We are just floating here.

KAREN: Why the multiplication tables?

CRYSTAL: Something like one and one doesn't always make two. Things are not always clear-cut. Things are not always what they seem.

KAREN: What isn't as it seems, specifically?

CRYSTAL [crying]: It is about judgment, pride and ego. It is to do with the choice of the body. I am experiencing the large body, so I have the opportunity to let go of my pride, my ego and my judging behavior.

KAREN: What happens if you change that?

CRYSTAL: Now I am getting a purple onion. It's about taking the layers off. The layers come off once I have done what I need to do and let go of what I need to release. They are saying that we have started to take the layers off. All the past lives I have experienced have been part of that. I am getting flashes of those lives. Aslan is saying not to be afraid to ask for help.

I am seeing the onion in front of me with the body there too. It still has no head. I can see layers coming off the body, like taking off layers of clothing. The layers of clothing are from many different historical periods. It represents the different lifetimes I have lived.

Both my guides are saying I need to connect to them more often.

Now I am getting a short person. This person looks masculine in the face but the gender seems neutral. I see a pointy, goatee beard and the face looks like it has been painted silver. It doesn't look like flesh.

This place is all multi shades of grey, like a deep, purply black. I don't like to say what it is. It is a planet, not Earth. It is hard to describe but the grey is bright and beautiful and calming. These colors don't exist on Earth. There is silver throughout the place. That is how the brightness comes through the purple, grey and black. The houses are shaped like upside down egg cartons. They are domes. And there are clusters of them.

The male-faced person has a mirror. He is holding it. It is a very large mirror. He is looking into it and then he turns it towards me. I don't want to look into it.

KAREN: But you're going to, aren't you? Are you looking into it now?

CRYSTAL: No.

KAREN: What stops you?

CRYSTAL: It is about facing up to reality.

KAREN: What would the reality be?

CRYSTAL: When I think about my past lives I think about how horrible and cruel I've been. The man with the mirror is actually showing me that my lives are far more balanced than

I thought. For every bad thing there is a corresponding good thing. He is telling me I am still judging myself even though I know that I had to experience it all. He is saying I need to let it all go. He is showing me hands ripping up a piece of paper, then opening the hands and letting the pieces of paper drift away into the wind.

I am not a murderer, I am not a rapist. I am not a child molester.

I have been raped several times. I have been murdered several times. I have been molested several times.

He is saying I just need to stop being so oversensitive. Let it go. I am writing it all on a piece of paper. 'Molester, victim, rapist, victim, murderer, victim.' Now I am ripping it up and letting it go. It is a whole feeling of unworthiness. I am not good enough. Nothing possibly good could happen to me. I don't deserve it.

I have thought of having a tattoo put on my wrist to remind me. I have thought of it for a while. It is a dove with a ribbon in its mouth. On the ribbon is written, 'Let it go.'

KAREN: Can you imagine seeing this on your wrist to remind yourself to let go?

CRYSTAL: I have seen this before but I keep forgetting to do it. Just like I keep forgetting to let it all go. All my life I have the feeling of not being worthy. I thought everyone was better than me. It came from my parents. They compared me unfavorably to others. But I already carried that feeling of unworthiness. Every time they made comparisons, I felt it confirmed how inferior I was.

KAREN: What would stop you remembering to let it go?

CRYSTAL: The old voices saying, 'You're not worthy. Why bother?'

KAREN: Whose voices?

CRYSTAL: My father's. You know, my guides are very keen for me to get past this.

KAREN: What do they suggest you do to get out of staying in this unworthy victim place?

CRYSTAL: I get a sense that it is easier to be negative than positive. If you are negative, people don't bother with you. They leave you alone.

KAREN: Why is that important?

CRYSTAL: People want things from you. Do this. Do that. Everybody wants something.

KAREN: So you don't like having people near you?

CRYSTAL: I love being with people. It is because I can't say *no*. Even when I say *no*, I renege and say *yes* later. Until I can say *no* and mean it I am stuck with unworthiness. It is a vicious cycle. I am unworthy so I have to say *yes* but when I say *yes*, I feel unworthy. It is a spiral.

After Crystal comes out of the trance, she says she going to tackle her lack of assertiveness. She wants to lose weight and be healthier. Now she knows what she needs to do.

Crystal faced some serious health challenges a couple of years after her session. She was in and out of hospital and couldn't walk for a long time. Twice I chanced upon her at the city hospital when I was visiting ill relatives. Crystal was in great pain and she faced it bravely.

We had spent many sessions coming to terms with her guilt, most of it from her past lives. In our last session, about a year ago,

I was delighted to discover she had let most of her guilt go. What a strong soul she is, signing up for such a challenging life.

Conclusion

The idea that we choose our body would seem extremely strange to most people. Most people think they *are* their physical body. They have no idea that their body is not an accident; that it was chosen by their soul-self for specific and important reasons.

From the cases outlined above, we gain a glimpse of the process involved in choosing our bodies.

Morris's experience demonstrates how much care we take when choosing our body. It must suit the purpose and challenges we have chosen for our life.

As Nadia's example makes clear, our physical self can be in conflict with our soul-self. We, as physical beings, do not fully understand the important role the type of body we choose plays in fulfilling our life's purpose. For example, we might have signed up to resolve conflicts and issues that have come down our ancestral line.

Crystal's case demonstrates how we may choose our body as a path of redemption for guilt accumulated over many past lives.

Once you know why you chose your body you are less likely to take it for granted. Once you appreciate its important role in fulfilling your life's purpose, you can be at peace with your body.

Meeting Loved Ones

Death is nothing at all. I have only slipped away to the next room. I am I and you are you. Whatever we were to each other, that we still are.

HENRY SCOTT HOLLAND

There is nothing quite as reassuring as meeting our loved ones on the other side. It can make a profound difference to our lives.

My grandfather died when I was thirty. He suffered from Parkinson's disease for over a decade. We watched this tall, capable, proud man wither away. He couldn't speak or communicate, although his eyes remained bright and alert. He shuffled and, when my grandmother fed him, he dribbled. Understandably, she became annoyed and impatient with him at times, and I felt his humiliation.

After he passed, I was haunted by the memory of his suffering—locked in his body, unable to express his thoughts or his needs. Sometimes, as I walked through town, I would see elderly men whose gait reminded me of my grandfather. Each time, I felt a pain stabbing at the center of my being.

Then one night he came to me in a dream. Actually, it wasn't a dream like other dreams. I was awake and asleep at the same time. I didn't understand at the time, but I know now it was a lucid dream. I asked him what it had been like being trapped in that failing body. He smiled. 'It was fine,' he said. I felt his joy and his love. He was perfectly at peace.

From that moment on, the ache I had suffered was gone,

never to return. I was puzzled. How could all that pain, years of yearning and sadness, be taken away so simply?

I was astounded at the transformation in me and I never forgot that powerful experience that probably lasted no more than a minute.

It didn't happen in a regression, but my waking dream resembled a regression in many ways. During a regression we are lucid and present, while our focus is directed to other realms. We report what is happening, which helps us remember. But profound experiences, like feeling the love and acceptance of someone we adored, cannot be forgotten. They live on like a light inside us, leading us forward with a renewed feeling of peace, and with a clear sense that all is well.

Most people who regress to their life between lives visit loved ones who have passed. Sometimes such contact has a transformative impact on the individual's life. Here are some cases that illustrate a variety of experiences of people meeting loved ones on the other side.

Ulrika

Ulrika came to see me because she felt trapped in Australia. She and her husband were from Germany. He was the one who wanted to come to Australia. As an engineer, he found it easy to get a job. Although the move was supposed to be temporary, he liked Australia so much that he wanted to stay. Ulrika loved her husband but missed her family back in Germany. She felt sad for her parents because both their daughters lived in other countries. She realised she was starting to develop a grudge against her husband. She wanted to find a way to be at peace. She thought a past life might show her the way forward. She'd been feeling very stuck and bitter.

Ulrika mentioned during our initial discussion that her grandmother had chosen her name. She had been named after her grandfather, Ulrich. He was a lovely man who had died before Ulrika was born. The grandmother herself had died when Ulrika was sixteen. Ulrika loved her dearly and carried her photo in her wallet.

Ulrika asked to experience a past life that would show her how to navigate her current crisis.

In the first scene she is a young woman in her twenties, wandering around in a large meadow. She is dressed in shorts, top and sandals. She is looking for someone. She wonders where all the people are and feels a strong sense of being lost.

I am getting a bit stressed. Where is everyone? Where are they? I hear someone saying I didn't follow directions and I got lost. I went the wrong way and got confused.

We move on to another scene, hoping to find some understanding. Now Ulrika is a woman wearing loose black cotton clothes. She is standing in a huge room beside a table. There are about twenty people watching her from some distance away. She cannot identify their faces.

I am scared. I am alone. I have feeling that I have done something wrong. These people are staring at me but I don't want to look at their faces. I am afraid to go towards them. I want someone to take me away from this room.

Now I am walking towards them. There is no other way

out. They are slowly moving out of my way. I am stepping outside. It is a very bright day and the light blinds me. I cover my eyes. I can't see things. I have stopped; I've frozen up. I feel very lost. I want someone to guide me and get me out of here.

We move to another scene. This time Ulrika is in a busy city. People pass her by but they do not seem to notice her.

I am crying a lot now. I need to calm down and pull myself together and get out of this mess. I am so lost I cannot remember how I got here.

I ask Ulrika if she wants her guide to come and help her. She soon senses a comforting presence at her side. Her guide is wearing a white robe and hood. She doesn't know whether the guide is male or female. The guide takes her hand and leads her along a path.

The hand is gentle and old, wrinkly and comforting. I am following the guide. It is daytime and it is beautiful and green. I am recognising the hand. The rings on the hand are the same as my grandmother's. I call out for her and she turns and I see her.

Ulrika is now crying.

She passed away when I was sixteen. She is taking me to a safe place... I can see my grandfather. He is so happy to see us.

We are hugging and embracing each other. I am very happy. My grandfather has kissed my forehead. That is the way my husband embraces and kisses my daughter. I wonder about this. 'It's the love,' my grandfather tells me. 'It is love that your husband has for his daughter. Unconditional love. The same love I have for you.'

So finally, I have met my grandfather. I have never seen him in my life. He is very lovely. We are so happy.

Ulrika weeps freely as she experiences her grandfather's love. I give her some time to enjoy this highly emotional reunion before suggesting that she ask her grandparents why she had been feeling so lost.

My grandparents look at each other and smile when I ask this question.

My grandfather is saying that I am trying to find myself. I don't know what I am doing and I am trying to find happiness and peace of mind. That is why I experienced these scenarios where I felt confused and lost.

He is asking me to follow my heart and not think too much. He is saying I go too much into the details and difficulties of things. I am to follow my heart and do what I feel is right, more than what I think is right. If I am in a situation where my mind is saying one thing and my heart is saying something else, deep inside I will know the right choice. He says I spend too much time thinking and worrying and feeling stuck. I am to make a decision and move on.

My grandmother is saying that my husband is a nice person who loves me and who does everything he can for us. She is asking me what more do I want?

I feel reassured. I knew this, but when someone who I look up to confirms this, it is comforting.

She knows I worry about my parents, because I'm living

so far away from them. She is saying my parents are fine. They know how to look after themselves. I do not need to worry about them. They are there for each other. There is nothing more they can ask for. Now I am feeling a great deal of relief.

I am asking my grandmother about my past lives with my husband. She is telling me she is sure that I have had past lives with my husband.

Even though they are my grandparents from this life, they are hugging me like my parents.

Now I feel the love from my husband, but I have shut down and become bitter. Knowing that, I feel sad. I want to open up and be carefree and bring back some cheerfulness.

My grandparents are telling me my job is to support my husband and my support is very important. He needs my love and encouragement to succeed. This love between us is more important than what country we are in.

In my heart, I know my husband and I share a deep love. I'm grateful to my grandparents for reminding me of this. In my frustration with him I had diminished that love.

My grandparents have given me a sense of direction. My part in all of this has just been made clear.

After Ulrika came out of the trance she felt light and happy.

I could feel each and every moment and every step I went through. It is my first time being hypnotised but my visuals were very clear. In the beginning I was puzzled and felt so lost. But the conversation I had with my grandparents seemed so real. I stopped feeling lost. Now I know what I have to do.

Ulrika had a profound experience meeting her grandparents. She had not specifically asked for a meeting with them, so it came as something of a surprise. However, they gave her exactly what she needed. She trusted them explicitly, and they proved to be the perfect messengers for her. Ulrika was going right off-track with her life, becoming more negative and bitter. Her grandparents lovingly gave her the guidance she needed. Not only did she have a wonderful meeting with her loved ones, she also received the information she sought.

I contacted Ulrika recently, four years after her regression. She is now happily settled in Australia with her husband and children. Rereading this account moved her to tears. 'It's such a beautiful and pure honest moment to revisit,' she told me. Meeting her grandparents and experiencing the power of their love had transformed her marriage, and her attitude to life.

Oceana

Oceana's father died when she was two years old. Because she was so young, his death had little meaning for her. At the age of twenty she attended a retreat in Bali. During those six months, memories of her father surfaced, and she worked through her feelings of loss.

Eight years later she lost her mother. This affected her profoundly. Her grief manifested as anxiety, anger, and distraction. Oceana couldn't cope with her two young children. She needed her husband to help manage the day-to-day running of the household. She also yearned for his emotional support. Unfortunately, his fly-in fly-out job in mining kept him interstate for weeks at a time.

A year after her mother died, still struggling with her loss, Oceana comes for a life between lives regression.

She accesses a past life as a six-year-old girl. This experience brings her into communion with her departed father. She reports a series of vignettes, suffused with vivid imagery and compelling emotions.

> *I am in a field on a sunny day, picking sunflowers and enjoying nature. I can smell bread being baked by my mother who is in the house with the baby. It gives me a feeling of being warm, safe and comfortable.*
>
> *I see Dad arriving home in his old-fashioned car and I feel so much joy. He is running to me and hugging me and twirling me around. He shares the same soul as my dad in my current life. His love is so powerful, I can take it with me, this feeling of love that is so huge.*
>
> *I can see it all so clearly, the rounded car and the little cottage.*

When I transition Oceana to another scene, she goes to an earlier life, which draws her closer to her mother. This time she is five years old, lying in a wrought-iron bed in the family's home.

> *I am very ill, very small, very thin with little stick legs. The room is familiar and comforting but I am very tired and weak. My mother holds my hand. I sense that she shares the same soul as my mother in my current life.*
>
> *I am seeing a bright light, and everything feels as it should be. It's funny to be dying and feeling so calm. It's sad for those left behind but fine for me. The light is bright and flickering and I feel that it's calling me.*

Now I can look down and see my body with my mother crunched over me. She is sad and crying, while I am feeling warm and fuzzy.

Oceana ascends and is greeted by members of her soul group. They envelop her in the warmth of their love.

My maternal grandmother is here and I am feeling the love from her. Now all the souls are there who have passed away in my current life, my mum, my dad and my grandma. They circle around me, letting me know I am safe and loved. [Tears fall from Oceana's eyes.]

Next, her guides approach. They reveal some hidden truths to her; truths that have the power to change her perspective on life, and on her grief.

I sense my guides around me now, telling me to look below. I can see the whole world below me and I am receiving a strong sense that the world is full of love, not heartache. Earth is such a loving beautiful place, it is like magic. I can see how we all get too caught up in all the things that are happening externally, the news, the disasters and all the things that don't matter to us personally and that are not even related to our life.

Apart from losing my mother, there is little suffering in my life. Losing her is part of my path. It is teaching me how to cope with great loss. I have such huge love from my husband and children and that will get me through, as well as the sup-port from my soul family who have my back.

I feel my dad's energy close to me now, his love. It is the same love my husband gives me and my daughter. I am part of a family now on Earth. It warms my heart when my husband comes home and twirls our daughter around like my dad did with me in the sunflower life.

I feel my mother holding me, surrounding me with love. I am learning that it was her time to go. She had done enough, and losing her is a test for me. I left her in that past life when I was five and she left me in this life. I was fine and I get that she is fine, too.

My father passed to help my mother grow, and me too. We both are learning these lessons about grief and my past lives were part of my learning. Now he is back, sharing the same soul as my daughter. He is going to have a longer life this time.

After the session, Oceana writes two long emails to me. She reports how much her life has changed after meeting her passed loved ones, and receiving so much information about her purpose. Here is an extract:

I feel so much better, so different and so happy with my family, my dear husband and my darling children. I still shed tears for my mum but that is natural and a part of it, but I can cope now and that is the difference. I feel like super-mum again with my dear children and not at all impatient and on edge like I was the past few months. I feel lots of inner calm and peace.

I got so much from my past life with my dad. I didn't even go into the regression thinking about losing him as a toddler. And yet I experienced such a deep healing from him and so much joy knowing his soul has incarnated as my daughter.

Oceana's case demonstrates the life-changing consequences that flow from meeting our soul family on the other side. Her experiences during the session are impossible to fully convey. Her words help, but there is nothing as powerful as feeling, in every cell of your body, the unconditional love of a close relative who has passed.

Sonya

Sonya has experienced much loss after her marriage. She gave birth to a baby at twenty-nine weeks, and named her Rachael. Rachael only lived for four months before she died. Later, Sonya became pregnant again, but miscarried at eleven weeks. She eventually carried two babies to term who survived, and lavished her attention on them. Her sons are now in their teens. Her losses were not the reason Sonya sought a regression. She had other issues she wanted to address.

Before proceeding to her life between lives, Sonya accesses a past life as a young woman called Victoria, in the nineteenth century.

Victoria is married to a man of considerable wealth, living in a large, well-positioned home. She has a son who she loves dearly, but he becomes ill and dies at the age of eight. While heartbroken, she doesn't grieve. Instead, Victoria becomes angry—angry with fate that her little boy was taken, angry with anyone who seems happy while she remains trapped in her pain.

Sometimes I feel like killing my husband and his parents. I don't understand them. I don't know how they can move on so quickly.

With more questioning, we find out they didn't really move on that quickly. They grieved for twelve months, but years later Victoria still feels bitter about losing her son.

I think about killing myself every day. I think about throwing myself off a cliff or under a train. I ride my horse so hard it's a wonder I don't fall off, and I wouldn't care if I did.

Her husband and family find her difficult to deal with. Eventually, she shuts down emotionally. She feels neither happy nor sad. She is simply numb. When her time comes, she is pleased to leave. She dies in her fifties.

During her meeting with the Council, she comes to several realisations. She didn't know how to express her feelings to her husband. She felt devastated by her loss, but she didn't know how to grieve. Afraid to feel the pain of losing her son, she instead became angry. Her suicidal thoughts calmed her, and helped her cope. She had to shut down emotionally to survive because otherwise she could have gone mad. The purpose of that life—and her current life—is to learn how to deal with loss.

Her guides take her to meet her soul group. After reconnecting with several people, she suddenly starts weeping.

She cries so profusely she can hardly get her words out. 'It's Rachael…'

Sonya weeps for nearly ten minutes. I know she is overwhelmed with the emotion of this unexpected reunion. Eventually, she cries herself dry, and finds her voice.

Rachael is an adult, such a beautiful young adult. She is wearing a robe and looks like a Greek priestess. I have such a strong connection with her. She is telling me I lost her three times. She was the child in that past life and she was the mis-carriage and the baby I lost. She is not used to the heaviness of the Earth energies and finds them very challenging. It was planned that she would leave early in both that past life and my current life. She is getting used to the Earth energies and I am learning how to deal with loss.

It is funny I called her Rachael. I found out later it means 'innocent.' She is telling me she chose the name she wanted, and sent it to me.

They are telling me that I am learning to blend the earth energies with the spiritual energies. It is all about loss, loss of loved ones. On Earth we think the person who died is dead and that the connection is broken. In the spirit world we know that isn't true. We don't really die and our energy is still connected to each other. Even if we are unaware of the conn-cection, we are always connected.

It is now coming to me that I haven't really dealt with loss in my current life either. I didn't grieve the loss of the babies that died. I got pregnant soon after and focussed all my attention on them. That was another way of distracting myself from the pain.

In both her past life and her current life Sonya feared fully feeling her loss, so she kept finding ways to avoid it. In her past life, she held herself together by shutting down emotionally and becoming numb. If she hadn't, she might have gone insane, given the depth of her grief.

By relaxing into the trance and experiencing that past life, Sonya created an opening for herself. She was finally able to grieve her losses. She discovered that avoiding grief resolves nothing. Grief is a form of energy. If unexpressed, it lies dormant within our psyche, waiting for the day when we are strong enough, open enough and wise enough to release it.

Wayne

Three months before Wayne embarked upon his life between lives session, his young brother had committed suicide. There were several reasons why Wayne wanted to undertake the regression—he had a number of physical and emotional health problems—but an important one was to see his brother. He had spoken to me just a month after his brother died. As he was still grieving, I suggested we give it more time. After giving it much thought, he agreed to delay the session. There was a reason why I believed giving it more time was important, and this case will illustrate why.

During his visit to his life between lives, Wayne was guided to the Council of Elders.

I am being welcomed and told it is a place of peace and learning. I have asked if I can see my brother but I am told that some others want to see me first. There are two cats who were members of our family. One of the cats is here now, Achilles.

Achilles wants me to know that there is nothing more I could have done for him at the end of his life. I am to stop thinking about his death and think about when he was alive. He wants me to know he loves me very much. He is purring and rubbing right up against me and doing all the affectionate things cats do.

Now Achilles is gone.

191

There is another cat here named Samson. He has no particular message. He just wanted to say hello. He is doing what he used to do when he was alive. He is sitting beside me with a very interested expression on his face. He is letting me know that he wanted to see me. He loves me and misses me, and the rest of the family. He is very happy. He misses the interaction he used to have with us. He liked all the affection we gave him and he gave us. He also enjoyed playing and teasing. It was a unique relationship. He is looking forward to seeing us again. He is going to hang around here with his interested expression while I am with the Council. He likes being around me.

I feel like my father is moving close but he is not here. Still, I feel his presence. He is not coming in because he is moving to another incarnation. It is all to do with him. He is not able to give the proper attention to what is happening here. His energy is focused on his new life. I am getting a sense of him being a teenager. He is very much engaged with the energy of that new incarnation right now and he is not able to engage with me.

It is disappointing but understandable.

I am asking if my brother can come. But I don't think he can just yet. Perhaps he will come later in the session.

The Council invited Wayne to ask his list of questions. I read them out for him, deliberately leaving the question about his brother until last. His mother hoped that the session would prove that her son was still alive on the other side. She was hoping for a specific message from him. The question that Wayne had framed for the Council was: 'Is it possible to interact with my brother?' This is what Wayne was told.

My brother can give messages at this time but he cannot come here. I am worried that my mother may not receive the confirmation she needs, and this worry is blocking me.

There is a message about his childhood that he is trying to get across. It is something to do with Christmas. [Wayne pauses.] *I have a terrible pain in my chest... It is grief.*

I suggest that Wayne allow this pain to dissipate by giving it lots of space. This does not eliminate the pain, although it eases a little at times.

I think my brother is referencing the ties that we had as children when we grew up together. Even after he grew up and started a family of his own, he still felt he was part of our family: me and mum and dad and our other brother. Even when he was away, he always felt that home was a place of safety. He knew that he could come home whenever he was truly in need.

I'm getting a lot of physical pain in my chest—so much that I have to stop.

I got the sense from the Council that I am not psychologically ready to let go of that pain. It would be like letting go of my brother. I am letting go but I am doing it by increments. The other reason is the sense of grief acting as a crucible. The loss of my brother is forcing me to change and make difficult decisions. It is helping me move forward and helping me grow. The sense of loss is helping me.

Wayne came out of the trance satisfied that he had received some genuine information from his brother. He had anticipated an emotional reunion, but his grief was too raw. Before he could interact with his brother, he needed to move past his intense grief. He was simply not ready.

He was pleased to know his brother's death is having a healing effect on his life. He sees this great loss as a wake-up call. He is starting to make important decisions that will address his psychological and physical problems. I suggested it was a gift from his brother. Wayne agreed and said he wanted to use that gift wisely and graciously.

He said he intended to allow his grief to heal more fully. Afterwards, at some point well in the future, he hoped to visit his life between lives to contact his brother.

Conclusion

When I do a regression, I only guarantee one thing: that the client will get what he or she needs.

Ulrika, in the first case, did not expect to see her grandparents. She only wished to find the answer to her dilemma. She felt great joy when her grandparents appeared. Because she trusted them unconditionally, their presence helped her accept and integrate their wise advice.

Oceana not only saw her mother during the session, as hoped, she also met her father and grandmother. This reunion made a huge difference to her daily life, putting her back on track and able to love and appreciate her family.

Sonya healed many losses during her session. She met the soul of the babies she had lost. She also learned that the losses were planned, designed for the higher good of both her and the babies.

Wayne desperately wanted to interact with his brother but

his desperation worked against him. Any negativity, even grief, can block the flow of information in the higher realms. He was shown, however, that connection with those who have passed is possible. This was demonstrated by the appearance of his two deceased cats that both expressed love for him and his family.

Wayne was also open and sensitive to the loss of his brother. Seeing his brother at this stage of his grieving may have been overwhelming.

I have had other clients who came to see me soon after losing someone precious. In most cases, they did connect with their loved ones. One mother lost her children in an accident and both children came through during the life between lives. I noted that she had not grieved, feeling emotionally shut down. The children coming through opened her up emotionally.

The desire to connect with loved ones is a legitimate objective in our life between lives. And although our desire is usually honoured, there is no way of knowing for sure whether the loved one will appear. All we can really know is that whatever happens is for the highest good of all.

When the loved one does appear, I regard it as a great privilege to be present. Observing a client connecting with a loved one is a poignant experience for them and also for me. Quite often I find tears welling up in my eyes while tears are flowing down the cheeks of my client.

I have some idea what they are experiencing. During my regressions, I have felt so much love flow into my heart and body that it overwhelmed me. It is an amazing feeling of coming home, of being completely cherished and accepted. Having experienced such intensity, I cannot help but sense the joy in my clients as they make these connections, especially since the connections are often with loved ones who they thought were lost to them.

Off Track

It is by going down into the abyss that we recover the treasures of life. Where you stumble, there lies your treasure.

JOSEPH CAMPBELL

Many people come to do past life and life between lives regressions because they want to know if they are on track with their life's purpose. Some feel unsure, lost or doubt themselves. Others feel quite depressed, with a few having suicidal thoughts. Some know they are off track because their life is a mess, or because they are facing a health crisis.

All sense that something is not quite right. They come to visit their life between lives hoping it will help. So far, in my experience, the clients who come in seeking guidance are given the answers they need. They receive clear instructions to help them get back on track. They are also given insights into their problems and advised how best to stay on track.

Joel

Joel, who is nearly forty, has been diagnosed with chronic alcoholism. He has experienced bouts of pancreatitis and a mild heart attack. His doctors have told him he will not live long if he doesn't stop binge drinking.

Joel sought a regression to discover why he needed to drink, and how he could attain sobriety. He was one of those people who knew his life needed to change.

On the way to his life between lives, we regress back to Joel's childhood. At the age of nine, Joel and his friend skip his Boy Scout meeting to go to an amusement parlour. Joel didn't mind Scouts but he found doing something illicit much more exciting. When he re-experiences this incident during his session, Joel feels a rush of adrenaline. It is so intense that he takes a few minutes to breathe through it.

We continue and Joel moves into a past life as James.

> *I am wearing ragged shoes and standing on cobblestones. A horse-drawn wagon is coming along the street. I see my uncle. He yells at me, 'Boy, what are you doing here?' I tell him that Pa knows I am here. It's a lie. Pa doesn't know. I am not supposed to be here in the town street.*
>
> *I am standing outside a shop. There is something inside that I really want. But I have no money. I don't know what it is yet but I really want it. I am thinking about stealing it.*

With my encouragement, James finally identifies the object of his desire.

> *It is a puppy. Now I see a sign. There are puppies for sale in this store. I would like a puppy to be my friend. I am angry with my father because I know he doesn't want me to have a puppy.*

We move to another scene in Joel's life as James. Well-dressed at the age of thirty-two, James is in a neatly-furnished drawing room asking a younger woman, Elizabeth, to marry him.

> *I am not getting a good feeling about this arrangement. I am not doing it for love. I am doing it for success, to get into this*

family. It is a well-respected family. Trouble is, her father won't allow it. I have made a mistake. I said something to him about wanting to be better than him and wanting to have what he has. She says, 'My father won't agree. He knows what you are like.' Basically I am using her.

I am disappointed. Life has been pretty routine up to now. But now, after meeting Elizabeth, I have become ambitious. Now what she has said is killing my dreams.

We move forward in time to another significant event.

There are two realities coming to me. One, I want to push away and just give up. The other is I go and talk to him and try and convince him.

James decides to talk to Elizabeth's father. He tells him how he will make sure his legacy is carried on and how he will look after Elizabeth. Eventually, her father agrees to let them marry. We move on to another scene in James' life.

Her father gets really ill. But I am not ready. I doubt myself. I am getting a strong emotion of self-doubt. Elizabeth says, 'You can do it.' She reminds me that I have been running the business. She believes in me.

I pause to allow Joel the time he needs to process the strong emotions that are arising.

Here I am at another crossroad, the same crossroad of self-doubt—like when I nearly gave up on marrying her. Do I give in or do I go on? [Joel pauses.] *I feel I gave up.*

Joel experiences a rush of painful emotions. I can hear the anguish in his voice as he looks back on this previous life as James.

I feel deep, deep disappointment. I am thinking, 'You almost did it. Almost played it out. Almost had everything you wanted. Then it got hard and you let it go. Gave up on everything you wanted to build. Just doubted yourself. It was there for the taking.'

I lost everything and I see a picture of me in front of the pet store. How much I desired that puppy.

Desire was still there somewhere but I gave up. I gave up on life and turned to alcohol.

I have a funny image of an old man. He's not really old, but he certainly looks old. He died lonely, disappointed and unhappy. I can see him [James], *in that alley, with a bottle drinking himself to death. He is in his late thirties.*

I support Joel as he moves away from the body, encouraging him to release his disappointment. He lets go with long, deep breaths. His guide, a male energy, appears and greets him.

He is asking me what happened. I say, 'I tried.'

He says, 'You tried and failed again'. I am asking how many times I have done this before. He is saying, 'Too many times to remember.'

There is a sense of disappointment in him.

He is saying that I cannot give up on myself or give up on life. 'You have to have another go. Get yourself ready for another life. You have people who love you. You need to work on it. It is not an easy journey. Some of these people have been with you before.'

I need to work with them. They will understand. Eliz-

abeth in James's life is my current wife. She is not going to leave me now. She is sticking to me.

He says I am to lean on people more. Stop trying to do it yourself because you can't. You tried. Be honest with people. You have to tell people who you are. You can show people your strengths. Tell people sometimes that you are struggling and they will assist you. You don't have to put on a façade.

I am scared to be myself. I don't know how I will go in another life. I don't know who I am. I can feel how closed off I have been. I am afraid to open to love.

Joel is taken before the Council of Elders. He is worried. He knows he has disappointed them again. They seem stern at first but they soon put Joel at ease.

They know I tried even though they are disappointed.

I am getting the picture of myself at nine when I wagged Scouts. I like the excitement of doing the wrong thing. I am getting the message that overcoming obstacles, like the business I took over as James, is also exciting. I have too much self-doubt. I get caught up in doubting myself and I try to overcome that by acting big and successful but then the doubts come in and I give up. I just have to learn to believe in myself.

Joel starts to tear up. I give him some time.

They are telling me that they believe in me. I am getting a strong feeling of reassurance and love. They say that I need to focus on accepting and loving myself.

Joel is shaken by his session. He now knows that he was not only off track with his current life, he has been going off track in many lifetimes. He can see that he uses alcohol as an escape from the disappointment he suffers when he gives up. And he gives up because of his self-doubts.

He knows he cannot do it alone. He knows he needs to let go of his false pride and seek help.

A few years later, I catch up with Joel. His business is going well and although he struggles with alcohol from time to time, he definitely hasn't given up.

David

David's journey is one of the most interesting I have encountered in my regression work. I have used different parts of his story to illustrate certain points in previous chapters. He received evidence of his life as a monk in Prague when he researched the Counter-Reformation of the seventeenth century. He was given an overview of his past lives and could see how issues and habits in previous lives affected his later lives. He obtained an understanding of the big picture when he learned that neither winning or losing is important and that short-cut enlightenment is not worthwhile.

In this chapter we meet David again. Now we discover the reason he undertook his regressions in the first place, and why he received so much useful information. He was off track with his life's purpose and, even though he was only twenty-seven, he had a sense of this.

My primary intention is to understand my life's purpose. What am I meant to be doing? I would like more direction. There is always choice—sometimes too much choice. I have an

intuition to make a certain choice and do something different,
but I seem to end up the same place.

David had prepared seventeen questions to ask during his life between lives session, including 'Why am I visiting Karen today?' Before we get to the questions, we begin with his previous past life. The story opens in 1730. He is a thirty-four-year-old man called Simon.

It is nighttime and I can see a clock tower that dominates the square. I am dressed casually in a cap, brown pants and a coat. It is late summer and cool. Brick houses surround the square and I can smell smoke from burning firewood coming out of the chimneys.

I live in this town in Switzerland but I am only passing through the square. I am here waiting for something important. I have my papers with me and I am going to make an exchange and receive travel documents. I have been working as a labourer, delivering coal and chimney sweeping. It is hard, dirty work. I am tired of travelling from place to place. I want to go to Austria. I want to do something more technical.

Originally, I came from a village in Germany, where it was green and pristine.

We move along in time to another scene in David's life as Simon, now a clockmaker.

I get to Austria. I want to open my own shop. At the moment, I am working for someone to relearn the skills.

Eventually, I get the shop, although it took longer than I thought it would. Things are going well but I'm a bit bored.

It feels like something is missing. I am now fifty-three and single.

We move on to another scene.

I feel very old, in my eighties. I am in bed. I get a sense that I worked hard but I did not achieve what I came to do. I am near the end of my life. There is a nurse visiting me at home. I die in my sleep. I am still in my house but I realise I have died. I feel sad. It was a very lonely life.

I achieved some good things. I liked the shop and moving from labouring to a better life. That took a lot of effort. But I feel like there was more I was supposed to do. It was a long life with an opportunity that I missed.

It feels calming passing on. I am out of the body but still in the room. The room is old with lots of books in it. The furniture is dark but well-built and polished. I came with nothing and gathered all these solid, material things that I have to leave behind.

I am ready to go. I just got a tap on my shoulder. Someone is there telling me to get a move on in a humorous way. There is a light I need to go toward.

It's like I am being pulled into a tunnel. It is quite relaxing. It is getting easier to let go and forget. I get a sense of a cool and refreshing breeze as opposed to the stuffiness and staleness of the air in that room. I feel lighter and not as heavy as being on earth.

If I look around there are endless horizons and boundlessness. Like being in the ocean.

Someone is here...

He is an elderly gentleman with a big smile. He has a white beard and is wearing a white robe. It feels like there are other colours around me. He gives me a big hug.

David cries gently. He is very emotional as he gradually gets his words out.

It is bitter sweet. He is happy to see me. While he is happy with what I did, there were some things he wasn't happy about.

He held me in his arms as a greeting but now he is standing beside me with his arm around my shoulders. There is much to discuss.

David's guide takes him to meet his soul group. There is one person in the soul group who stands out, Mary. He is told that the importance of Mary will be discussed later. Then he is taken to the library where his past lives are shown to him in the pop-up book described in a previous chapter.

The book is open at the last page. On the left is the life of Simon and on the right is a blank page. There are rough sketches on the left page, while the lives presented on the previous pages are three-dimensional and vividly coloured. These previous pages represent the lives I lived before this life as Simon.

My guide seems frustrated. He needs to use an eraser to change the sketches on this left page. This page represents the plan we made for Simon's life. He says the plan was a continuation of the earlier life when I was Desmonte, the monk. 'You made the decision to run away rather than stay and take on the challenges. In your next life as Simon, you must deal with the consequences of that decision.'

The life of the monk was the first past life that David did with me. When his guide reviewed that life, David realised he had made the wrong decision. He ran away from Prague when life became uncertain and a bit tough.

I was given different routes... I am trying to work out what the theme was behind Simon's life. It was meant to be a more physical and material life.

I started on a farm somewhere in Germany. I can see myself doing all the farm things. Looking after livestock. I never got really involved with religion there, so that was a good thing. Times had changed anyway. I needed to subscribe to religion but I didn't have to turn up to their rituals.

I was meant to find a craft. And I did, later on in life, but I had started an apprenticeship as a watchmaker earlier on. I was meant to have a family in that lifetime. I was meant to marry Mary. I met her while I was an apprentice. It is like the business fell on hard times and I decided to move away and look for work. I felt sad about leaving Mary behind.

I can see what was supposed to happen and what actually happened. I am going back and forth between each. It was a crossroads. A decision point.

I am being shown that if I had stayed and married Mary it would have been hard in the beginning, but I would have found another apprenticeship in the town as a watchmaker. We would have moved eventually but we would have been together. At times, there would have been some economic instability. Watches were a luxury item. Most townsfolk used sundials. The clock tower I saw in the town in Switzerland was unusual. But the relationship with Mary would have been good. Our love would have gotten us through the hard times. We would have been happy together.

The page now has to be rewritten because I didn't follow what was supposed to happen.

Now my guide is telling me that we have to go.

I query this. 'What about changing the page of Simon's life?'

We will be coming back to fill in the blank page. Now I have to go and answer for the life I had [as Simon].

We are leaving the book and walking back through high-ceilinged corridors. We go into a chamber. It is grand and medieval.

There is a panel of people sitting at a slightly curved table. One is in the middle with two on each side. My guide makes six.

There is a spotlight where I am to stand but I haven't been told to go there yet.

They all look busy trying to get their facts right. They are peering at papers. They wear dark-blue robes embroidered with gold. Their faces are dark at the moment but I can still see my guide.

They are ready now.

I am before them in the middle, in the spotlight. The two on the left are female and the others are male. The Council members have different coloured auras. The two ladies on the left appear pinky-purple. The middle one is bright white and yellow. Of the two on the right, one is purple and one is white. They are not really showing a lot. They are there for guidance, not to tell me their life story.

The one in the middle stands up and welcomes me back. He says we have a lot to discuss. Then he sits back down.

The one on the far right says 'We are somewhat happy,' but the one on the far left says, 'We are disappointed.' The one on the near right speaks.

'You are good at keeping routine but that doesn't really work for you if the routine is bad in the first place. This interview is about you breaking old habits. This is the second time we have been here discussing the same thing. There is no excuse. There was a lot of time in between your current life and your previous life. You achieved much greatness in your first few lifetimes.

'It is good that you lived in the material world this time, but there was more you needed to achieve. You were trying to survive. You made a rational decision but that decision was not the best. Keep it in context and think about the pain your decision brought to others.'

He is especially referring to Mary.

'She died young after becoming sick. You would have been better off together. It was good that you got away from the religious enclaves. Mary was there to help you achieve your plan. She left early because you decided to move away.'

I am asking them, 'How do I know when to stay and when to go?'

'You have got to trust your intuition,' they tell me. 'You hear it but you do not listen to it. Your circumstances were favourable, so you could have stayed. There were people around you who would have helped. You left and had nothing anyway. So you ended up worse off, and that was really stupid.

'It doesn't mean that if you follow the plan everything will be balanced in your favour, but there will be always be a wild card there to help.

'You ended up doing something you didn't want to do anyway. You became a labourer. Even after you achieved what you hoped and got your shop, it didn't mean much to you. That was because of the sacrifice you made in the first place.'

They are telling me that I did show kindness to others in that life as Simon. I ask what they mean and now they are showing me actions I took that were helpful to others. Those acts of kindness came from the choice I made. Having nothing made me compassionate.

My spiritual progression will not be an individualist approach as much as I would like it to be. My habit is to do things alone and that is not going to work.

They are telling me, 'Even though you did your best, we will keep sending you back until you get it right.'

The Council asks David if he has any questions about that previous life. I check David's list but these questions have already been answered. David is told to go back to the library to fill in the blank page and gain some more learning. He is told that he will be coming back to the Council again later.

We are there [in the library] *and my guide is sketching the blank page out.*

Now he is doodling on the page that relates to my current life. He is telling me I will find it easier to work with other people in my current life. There will be multiple choices and some tricky decisions but it is the same idea as the last lifetime.

It will be a materialistic lifetime. Family and wealth are both important. I am meant to marry and have my own family.

I didn't have as much choice in my previous life. In my current life, there are many ways of achieving my purpose. Some paths take longer than others. My guide has a timeline. He says I will reach various milestones at different points and in different sequences. There is choice.

It seems to be structured so I can break routine. It is not an individualistic enterprise. I need to work with other people around me. These people will help me achieve the wealth and family. He is stressing that the wealth and the family are interlinked.

There are various timelines and he is explaining the different paths. The fastest is the people path. It will be intuitive but it won't be a lonely path. It will be challenging because I haven't been on the planet for a good while whereas others have had multiple lifetimes in the meantime.

He said to keep in the spotlight. Don't become a recluse and the rest will fall into place. Also, listen to your intuition and act on it

He is asking me if I understand the plan. I do. He is keen I get it right.

Now David moves back to the Council. He laughs when his guide quips to the Council, 'He needs all the help he can get.' David goes silent for a while as he receives more wisdom from the Council.

They are reiterating what the guide said. They are making

sure I understand the plan. It is the same as before. They are reminding me that the circumstances are more favourable for the successful completion of the plan in this current life. Now I am being told to ask my questions.

The Council tells David he is doing the regression so he can remember why he is here and that there is an opportunity for change. They say, 'Get it right or you will be back in another lifetime doing it again.'

He is told he has the ability to read people and he developed a lot of courage in his first few lives as warriors. He lost some of that courage in his religious lives but in those lives he developed the ability to stick to a routine and has learned to be compassionate.

One weaknesses is his attachment to unhelpful routines. This is a double-edged sword. Even though routines can be helpful, at times David allows conventional thinking to override his intuition. What worked in the past may not work in the future. He needs to be more flexible at times.

He is told that isolation can work for you and against you.

If you look back to the life in Prague, your isolation was a strength but you lacked courage. As Simon, you had courage but isolation didn't work. Use your intuition to get the balance right.

The Council tells him he uses his intellect well. They are happy with the people he chooses to have around him. They are also pleased he is seeking guidance.

When David asks about his choice of career, he is told it could have been better. He chose a technical profession that is very isolating. They suggest he find a people role and study law, medicine or events management. 'With the skills you have you can be successful in any of those.' They note that he is young and has enough time to change careers. A humanitarian role will help him achieve his plan.

David then asked about travelling overseas. The Council issued him with a stern warning. He is not to travel before he is ready. In previous lives he ran away from his problems. Going overseas is not a matter of time but more a matter of how far he has progressed on his life path. If he gets the wealth and family at once, he can go whenever he wants. 'Don't go to a destination where you will have neither.'

The Council reminds David that he had a great sense of humour when he was a child. It is important to get that back. He won more hearts with it than he offended. They suggest he ignore any offended people anyway.

David is delighted with his session. Even though he is told, in no uncertain terms, that he is off track, he feels empowered to do something about it. Within weeks, he has enrolled in law at university, gone on a bush-walking expedition with a group of like-minded people, joined Toastmasters, gone out with his work colleagues, looked up some old friends and generally made an effort to talk to people whenever he gets an opportunity. He was told by the Council that he has not yet met his future wife. He knows he has to cultivate a robust social life to create the opportunity to meet her. He is absolutely determined to fulfil his plan this lifetime.

Savannah

Savannah, aged forty-seven, came for a regression to understand her life path. For a year, she had dated a married work colleague, Gerard, aged thirty-one. Gerard then ended the relationship with Savannah, left his wife and became involved with Peta, a woman of twenty-five.

Savannah is still deeply attached to Gerard. Although they remain friends, she wants more. She feels they are destined to be together and admits she is not getting on with her own life. She is angry, focusing her anger on Peta, the young woman in Gerard's life. She knows these feelings are irrational.

In the session, Savannah senses she was an Indigenous Australian woman. She finds herself near some large rocks, thousands of years ago.

I am on a rock, waiting for something or someone. It is Gerard. I heard him call my name. He is saying, 'But Sav!' Now I see he is staring at me. He wants me to see something but it hurts to see it. There is a part of me that doesn't want to see it. I am walking away.

He is putting his hand on my shoulder and he is very gently wanting me to look. But I feel like I am going to see the reason I am losing him, and if I see it, I will have to accept that I am losing him. I am a stubborn soul. I want it my way.

I have pulled right away from him now. I was about to dive into this valley with him and crash and burn. I feel like it has happened before and it is going to happen again.

Savannah hesitates. I suggest that stubbornness comes from fear, reminding her that she cannot blossom unless she opens to the truth. I ask her if she wants to understand why Gerard chose Peta, rather than her.

> *I am feeling something in my heart. It feels soft and wet and new, like wet behind the ears. My heart is delicate and vulnerable, but not fragile. I am wondering what am I going to see? He is standing behind me with his hands on my shoulders, feeling solid and strong. He has taught me about confidence and strength.*

Savannah now receives crucial information about the contract her soul made with Gerard's, before they incarnated. It seems they planned to wake up to their true selves in their current lives. It often takes a shock to wake us up. Peta's energy will rock Savannah to the core, and she is not going to like it. The confusion in Savannah's words shows how lost she feels.

> *I have to walk through some murkiness with him. He wants us to go through this together. It is a thick greyness, even black in parts. We have moved off the rock, walking through this thickness. Now we are coming to a clearing, looking down a valley towards the ocean, lit up, with the air clear.*
>
> *I feel like something is going to come out and shock me. We are just looking at each other and he is speaking to me. 'Remember how we said. We will work together.' He is pulling me in close to him so I get his intention. I am going, 'I am a bit doubtful?' Something is floating around me, behind me like an angry whirlwind, like a tantrum. It's Peta. She is affecting me more than him. He knows she is there and he knows it will hurt because I didn't want to do it this way. I wanted to do it a different way. But the destination is the same.*

I have to let go of the need to make it work my way. I have to let go of my emotional investment in him. I need to accept the reality, but I am struggling with accepting Peta.

I just need to accept. That acceptance is part of my path. The path is to not accept and then accept.

Savannah was not meant to be with Gerard this life, even though they are soul-related. His role in her life is to challenge her, to help her let go of her constant stubbornness. Being stubborn can be useful, but not in every situation. Savannah realised that by refusing to let go, she was off track. She needed to accept their romantic relationship was over.

After the session, Savannah was determined to put this relationship behind her and get back on her path.

A year later Savannah's relationship with Gerard is platonic. She is happy, absorbed in other activities and her career. She continues to work on her need to control, improving her ability to surrender to what is.

Liana

Liana is in her mid-thirties but looks much younger. She is intelligent, articulate and speaks quickly. I sense her nervous energy and wonder how easily she will relax into a trance. Luckily she has been successfully hypnotised twice before, to help overcome her anxiety.

Liana is interested in being regressed so she can find out what she is meant to be doing. She has an intense personal drive and tells me about her work history. She has changed jobs quite often because she becomes impatient and restless. She is achievement-oriented and gets bored easily. She is very keen to progress and be successful.

Once I understand Liana's background, I lead her through the trance induction. She transitions effortlessly into a past life.

I see the sun rising up behind the dark silhouette of a mountain, while I watch from the top of another mountain. It's such a peaceful, natural environment. Looking downwards, I see a gulch between the mountains. The sun paints the clouds in hues of orange. It is cold and I welcome the warmth of the sun.

Liana sees herself as a Mongolian man in his early thirties. She describes him as wearing a moustache, brown boots, a fur-trimmed hat and carrying a long knife in his belt.

Apart from my horse, I am alone. I am waiting for the morning light so I can embark on my journey. I ride down to the foot of the mountain, passing through green lands and villages on my way to my destination. I see a woman hanging out clothes. Now the clouds have cleared, it is a sunny day with a big blue sky.

I arrive on a plain where there are two rows of white tents. It feels like home but I am not sure. Each tent has a fire inside so the inhabitants can boil water and keep the room warm. I can smell the burning firewood.

I am at a tent where I see animals and a black Labrador dog. I go in and find the tent is quite small. A woman is preparing food. She is dressed in Mongolian clothes and has a ruddy face. She glances at me, then returns to her cooking. There is no welcome, no interaction. I am not a stranger to her or the dog but neither seems interested in me. There is an old woman sitting on a bench near the inside corner of the tent. She sees me but has no reaction. They are not upset to see me nor happy to see me. They just seem neutral.

I ask how Liana feels about the woman's lack of interest.

It is a numb feeling. I am not bothered. I am just observing these people.

I see a baby wrapped in white cloth that is made of hemp. I am in the tent with these three people, the woman, her baby and the grandma. They should be a family.

I am not staying. I am leaving. I feel no attachment to them. We are the same people and tribe but I don't feel anything for these women or the baby. I don't know if we are related.

Liana pauses briefly, before moving forward with her story.

Now I have switched scenes. It is nighttime. There is a boat on a lake at the edge of a cave. I can see a half-moon hanging in the middle of the sky.

I am on the boat. I am a Chinese man wearing the robes of an ancient dynasty. My name is Jade and I am in my early twenties.

I hear his thoughts asking, 'What can I do about this?'

I feel that he doesn't want to stay where he is. He wants to go somewhere where he can see the oceans and the mountains. This place is very nice, tranquil and peaceful but he wants to experience new things. He wants more. He is very much like how I feel now. He is not interested in seeing people so much; he wants to see the world.

We move to another scene in Jade's life.

He is getting old and wearing white. He found something that he wants to do. I sense a settled feeling in him. He is in a classical Chinese garden with a big house. He is facing me and behind him there is a wall, like a screen, made into a pattern with pebbles. Around there are green bamboos and a painting of ink on cream papyrus.

I got a key word, salt. He is in a business with salt. I think he created this business and this is his house. He is confident and he knows what he wants. He likes the freedom of having his own business. He is settled because he has achieved something.

At this stage in the regression, I have no idea if this is a past life or a symbolic meaningful scenario. I ask Liana what 'salt' means to Jade.

Salt means 'the elementary foundation'.

I see another older guy who is senior and superior to Jade. Now I feel he is the owner of the house. And there is a young lady who is this older man's daughter.

They should be a family.

I don't feel any attachment to the older man or his daughter. Perhaps Jade is an employee of the older one.

I find it hard to relate to people. I can only imagine myself. I cannot relate myself to them.

I ask Liana to call in her guide so we can understand what is happening.

I see a room with pale yellow walls because the winter sunshine is coming through the windows. There is a small cloud in the room that changes. It is The Lord of the Rings *guy. He has long white hair and wears a gown. I get the name, Teacher. He is talking but I didn't catch his meaning.*

I explain to Liana that she needs to open up to hear what he is saying because his words are challenging her belief system.

Now I get it. He said, 'They are your families. That is how you learn to love. You learn from the experience of having families. Both of them [the Mongolian man and the Chinese man] *were ambitious to do what they wanted. Neither of them paid much attention to their families.*

'You are doing the same thing in your current life. This has been a pattern in many lifetimes for you.

'Basically you need to learn to love yourself, then extend your self-love to those around you, and also accept love from others. You get the sense of belonging from loving yourself. You block and ignore your relationships with others because relating to them feels uncomfortable for you.

'Learn to accept yourself as you are through being, *rather than through* doing.'

He is turning to leave, but he didn't tell me about my career. I am chasing after him to ask about my career.

He seems annoyed with me. He says, 'You know why I left. That's the old pattern.'

I can see we are not going to receive any more information from Liana's guide. She is resisting his message. He knows giving her more information is pointless. Earlier in the session, she had relived an emotional moment in her current life when she was aged two. I now remind her of that experience and take her back to it.

I am sitting on my grandparents' sofa in their living room. I am against the window and I can feel sunshine coming in. Doors on the right-hand side of the room lead to two bedrooms, my grandparents' and my aunt's. On the other side, I see my grandmother sitting at a dark wooden dining table. Soon my uncle and my aunts will be coming home. They will join us for lunch and play with me. I am sitting there with my uncle beside me. He is the funny one. It feels like home. I have a strong feeling of belonging.

Liana cries. After helping her get further in touch with this feeling of belonging, I suggest she bring it back with her to the present. It needs to be integrated into her current life. I also remind her of her guide's message about loving herself first so she can love others, and accept love from them.

When she comes out of the trance, she laughs at her foolishness for chasing the guide. She realises she was missing his message. Liana has been off track for many lifetimes. She agrees that she doesn't know what love is and struggles to open up to her loving husband. I wonder if this session will be enough to open her eyes so she can start changing.

I talk to Liana a couple of months later. She tells me she has changed significantly. She took the notes home and read them at least four times. She decided to let go of her fears, uncertainty and self-doubts. She feels more settled and has stopped worrying about her career, and whether or not she should change jobs. Her focus is more in the present and her relationship with her husband is stronger. She is very happy she decided to do the regression.

Grace

Grace is in her late thirties. She asks to visit a past life that will bring her peace, both within herself and in her environment. While Grace is a writer, she hasn't written a word for twenty-two years. She knows she is meant to be writing, but tells me that the 'block is massive'. Even meditating for three years has not been enough to shift it. She says she knows her writer's block stems from feeling unsafe, and believes these feelings originated in a past life.

During the pre-brief before going into the trance, I also discover that she is an insomniac who has always carried a fear of being murdered. She is somewhat nomadic and barely stays in one location more than eighteen months. Several psychics have told her she is a restless soul, advising her that peace comes from the inside, not from the world outside. All her moving will not bring her peace. She has travelled to Third World countries to help in crises, and describes herself as having a 'rescue drama'.

Grace's background was emotionally and physically abusive. I ask her if she thinks her problems might be related to her personal history, but she is convinced they come from a past life. She mentions a dream she had as a child. A gypsy woman buries her alive. She recalls that her grandmother used to threaten that the gypsies would take her away if she misbehaved.

Grace goes easily into trance. As we move back in time, I ask her to participate in an activity she enjoyed at the age of eight. She reports that she is playing with friends in a playground. As she remembers a grassy patch nearby a shadow passes over her face, and her mood shifts.

I don't like this place. I feel like I am buried here. Someone is shoveling dirt on me and I can see them laughing.

I don't understand the significance of these images so I ask Grace what they mean. She shifts her perspective, answering as an adult.

I think it is from an earlier era. It could be symbolic. My life was most creative when I was eight. It was golden. Then mum got post-natal depression when my little sister was born. I was buried then and became the family slave.

Grace then shifts to a past life as a young girl. She is standing on the top of high cliffs, looking down over houses that stretch to the edge of the sea. Then she starts to run.

I'm racing over the grassy hills with the wind in my hair. I feel free. I am laughing. I am really happy. I don't know why but I am really, really happy. Just being myself. Being free.

The scene changes and Grace senses darkness. She feels she is clambering through a dark tunnel.

I am standing on a grassy field in England, in the nineteenth century. I wear a green dress with a grey shawl. I am twelve years old. Soldiers with helmets drag me by the arm across the grass. I feel like they are rescuing me. There are horses hitched to a cart. We have to go. There is no time to ask what is happening. We must move quickly because there is some immediate danger. A whip cracks, and we lurch forward.

I don't know why we must go quickly. I feel anxious, but

a lot of my anxiety is because I don't know why. No one is telling me why we cannot stop.

There was a wide clearing but now the road is narrowing and the woods are closing in on each side. It is growing darker and I have to sit low in the cart to avoid overhanging branches. Grey clouds are blotting the sky. I have an old blanket that I am trying to wrap around me tightly because it is very cold and the wind is biting into my cheeks. Luckily, I have a bonnet on my head. A soldier sits nearby but he doesn't say a word to me.

It is a long journey. In the evening we finally reach our destination. I am almost dragged around the back of a grey stone building and through a wooden doorway. Stone stairs wind upwards to a room at the top of the house. I am taken to this room where I am left, with the door closed and locked. The room is small, with a single wooden bed and washstand. I look out the window. There is a stone courtyard at the back of the building. A few people carry buckets or bundles on their shoulders. They are servants going about their business. The countryside in the distance is green and foggy. Rain is coming.

No one has told me anything. I am just going along with it. I am not feeling trapped because I get a sense I am being looked after.

A maid comes with food on a tray. Before I go to sleep I look through the window to the sky and the stars. The rain has washed away the clouds.

We move on to another scene in this life.

There is a lot of fighting around me. Fist fighting. It is not about me but I use my arms to protect myself. It is a pub. I have been living above a pub. Now I am down in the pub. Men are punching each other and things are being knocked over. I wedge myself under a table to get out of the way, as they are close to me. I don't feel afraid. I just go along with everything.

I go into the kitchen where the cook gives me some bread. She tells me to run over the hill to find a man with a black horse. I go. I see him now. He has a black hat and is coming towards me. He gathers me onto the horse behind him and turns away from the pub. I cling onto him as he gallops off. I know there is danger and people are after me.

We come to a ship moored in a bay. I am going on that ship and sailing somewhere. The man has left me there and ridden away. I am to wait. I am still wearing the same green and grey clothes.

On the boat, everything is much slower-paced. We have many days ahead of us on the voyage. Everyone is friendly towards me, including the Captain who has been charged with my care. He's a nice man.

I am going to Italy. Genoa. He has no idea why. A gentleman paid for my passage and that is all he knows.

I am very happy on the ship. I love the seagulls, the sea, the sun and its warmth. The warm sun feels miraculous to me. I have never experienced such warm sun, or such a refreshing sea breeze. I feel beautifully relaxed and comfortable and I am really enjoying this part of the trip. Even so I want to get to Genoa, to find out why I am on this journey.

I have just arrived. A family is waiting on the jetty, smil-

ing. A woman, a man and their son. Their arms are open and they are hugging me with tears of joy. I have never met them before but I sense they are relatives on my mother's side. I am to live with them. They are kind, loving people and I feel very safe with them.

I have come to live with them forever. They are my family now. I feel happy. It is nice to be with them.

Before I had a sense of being carried along. I had to keep on moving. There was a sense of danger. Now I see there was a plan to get me to this end point.

Now I am hovering in space. I am looking down at the Earth. I feel like I am in limbo. It is like a time out. I am getting some distance from my life as Grace. It is about finding perspective.

My inner voice is telling me to go home. You know what to do. Move to the beach. It doesn't matter which one. Be happy. Just be. Be happy.

I am being reminded of my guide giving me a sword. I have had this image before. I am to remember the rocks and the sword. It represents a message that I am always loved and protected.

My guide is telling me that love has always been waiting for me. He tells me there is a home that has always been ready to offer me sanctuary. People with open arms are there for me.

But open arms feel like a prison to me. I want to be the young child running up the hill, laughing. Now I am running up the hill, running free and forgetting that there is always a home for me. I get the message, 'Stop trying to be free all the time.'

I ask Grace: 'Why did the twelve-year-old girl feel so happy in Genoa with the welcoming open arms? And why does Grace feel like the open arms are a prison?'

'Fear,' she whispers. 'It is in my knees. My knees are locking up and hurting from fear.'

Grace becomes restless. She says she is getting a physical feeling of fear. She feels like she is shaking and crying. I can see she is greatly distressed.

I reassure Grace that she is safe and suggest she stays with the feeling to discover what is going on.

> *They are hitting me with the shovel. I am in the hole. It is my family who are doing it to me. It is another lifetime. They broke my knees first. I am female, aged seventeen.*
>
> *They hate me so much. They never liked me. They are nasty people. They want to kill me and they are killing me.*

I ask Grace to move away from her body, so she can observe what is happening and why.

> *I tried to tell them something they didn't want to hear. I bought shame on them. We are quite poor. We are peasants. They have hated me since I was little. I was my father's child. The woman is my stepmother. The brothers hate me. They have made me feel illegitimate. I can remember my father being kindly to me when I was little but now he is killing me. I have said things they didn't want me to say.*
>
> *It is all to do with local politics. I have said things against certain people in the village but I think they are just using this accusation as an excuse to do what they have always wanted to do with me. Now my father has given them permission*

226

because I have brought shame to him. He has turned his back on me and disowned me as his daughter. The stepmother is screaming at me: 'Filthy girl, filthy girl.' They pull my hair to get me into the hole. I feel their hate and anger. They broke my knees so they could drag me into the hole. I am seeing them doing it to me.

I wonder why I chose this experience? I feel like I have to be punished. I don't deserve to live. I feel worthless and unlovable. I am like a cuckoo in the nest. I am not supposed to be there. I am unwanted.

I need to learn how to love unconditionally. So I chose a life in which I experienced its exact opposite—unforgiving violence.

I can see the usefulness in that.

I ask Grace if she can let go of the horror of that lifetime.

Any love from my current family has been conditional. All my life, my mother screeches at me like a banshee.

I still seek my father's love. You know how that worked out in that past life. In my current life, my father is not reliable. His love is conditional. He has a lot of expectations of me that I try to meet. I need to have other people in my life but I have no friends. I feel very alone.

I tell Grace that we make friends through consistent contact. When we see people regularly, we get to know them. Some people will resonate with us, and we can ask to spend more time with them. As long as each person takes responsibility for continuing the contact, a solid friendship can develop. I pause before making the obvious point: 'It is hard to make friends if you keep moving.'

Grace emerges from the trance emotionally drained and physically exhausted. Even so, she feels a new sense of freedom. During our debriefing, she says she knows what she needs to do. She will move to the beach and settle there. She has some other realisations. If she wants to be free of her family, yet not alone, she needs to make friends. She knows she has never made lasting friendships because she has never stayed in the same place. She is not afraid of open arms anymore. She knows she just needs to discriminate between people whose affection is conditional and the open arms of those who are able to love unconditionally.

Conclusion

As these cases demonstrate, a regression can show you where your life has gone off track. It can also help release your fears, and offer you valuable insights. But a regression alone does not guarantee lasting change. To get themselves back on track, my clients need to take responsibility for shifting direction and applying their newfound knowledge to their lives.

Some people do a regression and then forget about it. They re-engage with their old habits. This is easy to do. To counter this tendency, I always suggest that clients take seriously any information that strikes a chord with them. For example, I type notes during the session so the client can take home an easy-to-read record of his or her journey. Soon after, I send them the audio recording of the session.

I am one of those people who makes notes of any insights I receive. When I was first regressed to my life between lives, I was given a recording on three CDs. Even though it took many hours, I typed up a transcript of my session. As I listened, I gained additional insights that I added. I put these notes by my bedside to read each evening until I had fully integrated the information into my life.

During that regression, I got a clear message that I was on track with my life. I realise now why that was the case. I wanted to learn and improve. At the time, I was not living my truth—not fully. I was still in the grip of some of my childhood conditioning. But I was on the way to dismantling old programs that had me playing roles others had scripted for me.

Being off track is as much an attitude as anything else. Your attitude determines whether you are progressing towards your purpose. David was off track but had the right attitude to quickly correct it. He had fallen off track in his past two lives. Now he was determined to change that and fulfil his purpose. He just needed to know what was required and he received that information.

Liana, on the other hand, had been off track in many lifetimes. Change might be more difficult for her. She had not really listened to her guide and was still focused on a societal definition of success. This changed for the better when she took the time to contemplate the wisdom behind her guide's messages.

Joel was going well when I last spoke to him but that was a few years ago. Overcoming an addiction is extremely challenging. I am sure we would be more understanding of addicts if we realised that they may have been struggling with their addictions over many lifetimes.

Grace continued on her journey of change and came back for further regressions to address other issues.

From conducting many regressions, I have come to the view

that our lives are planned. Our soul-selves meet with others to plan our lives. Then our soul incarnates like an avatar to put the plan into action. At this point, everything hangs in the balance. On Earth, we have free will. We are free to fulfil our plan, or to discard it entirely. Many obstacles and distractions compete for our attention. We encounter many temptations that can throw us off track.

Over twenty years as a counsellor, I have observed many people who found themselves off track. They are not happy. They come to therapy saying they are lost, depressed, anxious, unsure of their direction and struggling with procrastination and lack of motivation.

Once they have removed their blocks and feel they are back on track, they find themselves full of energy and enjoying life. Nothing, in my view, is as important as feeling you are on track with your life's purpose.

Redemption

We can be redeemed only to the extent to which we see ourselves.
MARTIN BUBER, PHILOSOPHER

Many of us harbour deep feelings of unworthiness or guilt. Usually we are not aware of these feelings as they are deeply buried in our subconscious. These repressed feelings are expressed in our day-to-day life in various actions and intentions. We want to be considered a good person. We have a desire to help others, sometimes being too giving and self-sacrificing. We feel so afraid and anxious at times that we fail to stand up for ourselves and allow others to put us down. Some of us might express our deep guilt and self-doubt by becoming hard and unforgiving. We hate backing down or saying 'sorry.' We might only feel safe when we are in control, and may resort to bullying others to maintain our authority.

These various behaviours are repressive strategies. We use them because we do not want to confront our guilt and sense of worthlessness. Somewhere along the line, we disconnected from these feelings and chose to keep them hidden. But these feelings unsettle us. Every now and then, they surface. At these times, we can become reactive, angry, anxious or depressed.

Some people then seek help. Such people are wise. Whatever the perceived reason for seeking help, what they really crave is redemption.

As you read on, you will encounter several people who felt burdened with guilt. Through the miracle of redemption, they found forgiveness, and a deep sense of inner peace.

Albert

Albert is in his early eighties. Albert approached me for a past life regression because he wanted to understand why he had faced certain challenges in his life.

The past life scene opens with Albert as a young boy wandering in the hills with only his dog for company. The young boy's name is Sam, and he has run away from home because his parents were arguing.

> I hate their arguments. My father is a hard man who is easy to anger. The sun is setting. I am going to have to go back even though I don't want to. I am coming closer to the house. I can still hear them fighting. My father opens the back door. He doesn't see me. He rushes out, slamming the door behind him. That is the last time I saw him.

We move onto another scene in Sam's life.

> My mother remarries. Although her new husband seems devoted to her, I don't warm to him. I am not yet eighteen, but I have moved away. I live on a farm and work for a kind-hearted farmer. I am happy here.

As the story unfolds, Albert realises that Sam is living in the nineteenth century, on the plains of the American Midwest. We move forward in time. Sam is at the end of his life looking back.

I am alone in an alley. Drunk. I am dying. I am about seventy. I bought the farm from the farmer. I loved the land and I loved farming. But drought came. Even though I had many good years, I was still in debt to the bank. I never married because I didn't want arguments like my parents. I started drinking. I couldn't pay my debts, and I lost the farm. I was about fifty when that happened. I wandered about the countryside seeking farm work. I lived the rest of my life as an itinerant worker. I kept drinking. I feel I have wasted my life.

Albert meets his guide who calms him after this disturbing realisation. We then explore parallels between his current life and the life of Sam.

Like Sam, Albert is a country boy at heart. He also abhors conflict. His father, like Sam's, was a hard man. In fact, Albert sees that his father shares the same soul as Sam's father.

Albert also shared the same vice as Sam. At the age of twenty, he started drinking. He drank heavily until age twenty-eight, when he suddenly realised that he was wasting his life. He then gave up alcohol completely.

Albert has handled the challenges in his current life much better than in the past life as Sam.

Like Sam he was afraid of relationships, but he overcame this fear and married. His wife and children have told him that he was hard and strict in the early years. However, he opened up and softened over time. He believes the partnership with his wife was one of the most stabilising influences in his life.

Albert has been better at decision-making than Sam. Albert learned to step back and reflect whenever he was struggling, and this has enabled him to solve his problems effectively.

In essence, Albert used the session to undertake a life review. Esoteric literature tells us that we review our life soon after we die. And it is true that people who have a near-death experience often experience a life review. Albert wanted to be at peace before he died.

After re-experiencing the past life as Sam, Albert feels very much at peace with the decisions he has made in his current life. He can see that he handled the challenges he faced in each life very differently. He overcame his tendency to escape through alcohol, and passed the tests life presented to him. He knows he has met the goals he set for his current life, and knows he will die peacefully, with a strong sense of achievement. He knows the mistakes he made in his past life have been redeemed by his actions in his current life.

Carlos

Carlos came to see me because he was experiencing fear, anxiety and guilt. He also felt insecure and inferior. He could find no reason for these strong feelings in his current life and he was sure they were connected to a past life.

Carlos went into the trance easily and the information flowed quickly—so quickly that he was taken to scenes from four different lives.

In the first life he is a Native American, prior to European settlement. He is hunting in the woods, stalking a deer. Drawing back on his bow, he brings the deer down cleanly, and triumphantly takes the carcass back to the tribe. He is highly regarded by the other members of the tribe for his hunting skills, and their gratitude feeds his pride. Although he has a wife and child, he pays them little attention. He feels no affection for them. Nearly all his energy goes into hunting so he can bask in the admiration of the tribe.

In the second life, he is a nomadic Arab roaming the desert with a small group of bandits.

The men in his clan live by attacking others and robbing them of their goods. It is a dangerous and brutal life, with much fighting and killing. The Arab has a very beautiful wife. Even though he is proud of having won such a desirable woman, he is jealous and insecure. He doubts her love and worries that someone will steal her. He doesn't really love her. Deep down, he feels he doesn't deserve her.

During his travels in the desert, he meets an old, wise man. He feels connected to this man in some way. This old man teaches him many things about life. He learns that fighting and killing are not good for him. He is told he could change for the better by finding a more peaceful life.

After listening to the wise man, the Arab feels confused and unsettled. He considers leaving his clan. He realises that if he leaves, he would have to abandon his beautiful wife. She has relatives in the clan and he would be in trouble if he took her with him. Even if he left her behind, her menfolk might still chase after him and kill him.

He decides to stay but he pays a high price. He is never happy or at peace. He spends the rest of his life feeling trapped. At the age of forty, he dies after by being knifed in the chest by one of the clan's victims.

In the third life, he is a warrior in a large tribe. The tribe admires his skills as a warrior, and the chief is very fond of him.

When he is thirty-three, a member of the tribe suddenly disembowels him in front of the chief and other tribal elders. The chief looks sympathetically at him while he is dying. But he sees the truth in the chief's eyes. He has done the wrong thing and he must pay the price. He slept with the wife of the man who kills him.

The warrior did not want to die. He was enjoying his life. But he made a mistake and the consequence was an early exit.

In his fourth life, Carlos is a blacksmith living in England in the nineteenth century. The blacksmith is eighty years old and dying of a heart attack. He looks back on his life.

I realise I am dead now and I am looking at myself on the bed. I feel I have wasted my life. It was empty. I still feel empty.

I was working hard all the time to forget about something. I wanted to keep busy. I made money but it gave me no enjoyment.

I wanted to forget about loss, the loss of a woman and a child. I killed them. I never trusted this woman. I thought she cheated on me and I didn't think the child was mine.

Now after I die, I know it was my child and she didn't cheat on me. But I thought she did.

I was not happy. I had a difficult childhood. I was an orphan and I survived by begging on the streets. There was no love and I felt worthless. But I wanted to move on and not be poor. So I got a job with a blacksmith and I worked hard.

The man I worked for was fat. But he was a good man who cared about me. Before he died, he gave the business to me. Being a hard worker is the only thing in life that I know how to do.

I met this woman. I think she liked me but I didn't feel love inside myself. Even though I didn't feel love, I didn't want to be alone. We lived together. It wasn't for long.

I killed her.

She was sleeping in the bed. I was insecure. I was angry with myself. I cut her throat with a knife. I want to be alone again. I don't feel love. I have no feeling. I burn the body and I throw the child on the fire alive.

I am dead inside. Numb.

Carlos is met by his guide. He reviews the four lives.

He sees how the Native American and the Arab focused on the admiration of others but felt no real connection to their wives or children. He learns that to be loved he needs to love others first.

He sees the strength in the warrior but he also sees that he looked for connection in the wrong place, with someone else's wife. He learns that to find happiness we need gratitude for what we have and to take only what is ours.

In regard to the life as the blacksmith his guide tells him, 'In life we need to face the pain instead of going numb inside.'

The guide takes him to a kindergarten where children are playing. He recognises one of the children as his present wife. This child comes to him and puts her arms around him. He sees that she is the child he killed in the fire. Carlos weeps as he realises how deeply he is loved.

Carlos has carried profound feelings of guilt and worthlessness into his current life. He is spiritual and seeks spiritual knowledge. He has a strong desire to help others and be a good person.

Now he understands why he has felt so much anxiety, guilt and insecurity.

He states that never in a million years could he imagine having a life like that of the blacksmith. He struggles to come to terms with the blacksmith's cold, violent acts, but he is on the path of self-forgiveness and is opening up more and more to love.

He recognises the great gift he was given by the child he killed in his past life. This child is now his wife. She loves him and he loves her. For Carlos, this gift of love is the source of his redemption.

Connor

Conner had an unusual reason for seeking a regression.

His wife had been to a psychic. The psychic had instructed her to bring photos of her loved ones to the reading. When the psychic picked up the photo of Connor, she exclaimed, 'He is all hung up.' She said he had been hanged in a past life and he was still hanging there. He needed to do a past life regression so he could be released.

Connor's wife didn't doubt the psychic. Connor so hated wearing neckties that he had even refused to wear one on their wedding day. She had also noticed that if she ever put her hand near his throat, he immediately recoiled.

When the session began, Connor passed easily into a trance. He finds himself standing on the cobblestoned colonnade of a colonial building, and immediately feels a sense of unease. In this life he in his forties, and he advises the Viceroy on matters of internal security. Or, to be less euphemistic, he is responsible for oppressing the native people, and maximising their productivity.

I sense that I'm living in the 1600s. Whatever county I'm in, it sure isn't European. The city has been built along European lines, but the hills are lush with tropical foliage. I'm wearing boots, brown leather trousers, a shirt and a vest. By my dress I'd guess I'm a man of some stature, but I'm also used to getting my hands dirty.

Connor enjoyed a warm relationship with the previous Viceroy, who has just been replaced. The new Viceroy does not trust Connor. There is some hostility there. Has Connor been too blunt, or insufficiently deferential? He treats the new Viceroy as an equal, as he did with his predecessor. But the new man has different standards.

In this city different races mingle. A number of European powers have business interests here. There are tensions between the people and their rulers, between the different merchants vying for advantage. The Europeans have drained the wealth from the surrounding countryside and live in constant fear of insurrection.

Connor realises that the native people lack the organisational skills and self-confidence needed to stage a successful revolt. Years earlier, he had served in a similar position in another colony. When the natives there failed to meet the quotas imposed by the Governor, Connor was sent in to discipline them.

I could be brutal at times. On the Governor's orders, I had the ringleaders hanged. This seemed to achieve the desired result, and productivity increased. But the people were choking back their anger. News of their unhappiness reached the Governor. He decided to make an example of me, hoping to win back the natives' trust. I was marched out into the square, in front of hundreds of people, and the campaign ribbons were torn from my jacket. Then I was shipped out. The memory of this previous mistreatment is fresh in my mind as I wait on the cobblestoned colonnade.

Connor learned from this experience. In his new role he tries to treat the local workers more fairly. He ensures that they have enough to eat. But there are other problems looming for him.

The old Viceroy retired because he couldn't balance all the competing interests in the city. As for me, I'm no diplomat. Those silver-tongued traders ran rings around me. And the new Viceroy is looking for someone to blame—someone a little lower down the pecking order.

There is some additional hostility between us because he is English and I am Irish. He sees me as inferior. He believes that I have been too soft on the natives, and that is why we haven't been meeting the targets set by London. He won't listen to me, and I'm not prepared to return to my old ways. I feel like I'm to be made a scapegoat.

Connor's sense of failure runs deep. He is waiting outside the Viceroy's office. He hears the Viceroy storming up and down, cursing Connor's ineptitude and calling for his dismissal. Connor cannot face another public humiliation. He retreats into the shadows, takes a rope and hangs himself from the rafters.

I ask Connor if he is ready to move on, but he is not able to leave his body. He is consumed with feelings of anger, guilt, humiliation and self-loathing. These are compounded when he overhears the Viceroy, who has been told of his death. The

Viceroy's fury knows no bounds. He rails against Connor, accusing him of cowardice in the face of censure.

I explain to Connor that this life is now over. There is no point being stuck in a dead body. He needs to release his negative feelings. I ask him to open up to see if someone is nearby, waiting to take him home.

Usually when I give these suggestions, a guide, a relative or a light being appears. However, the individual who arrives was someone neither Connor nor I could have anticipated.

I sense someone approaching. It's a black man—a slave. It is a man I had hanged.

Connor is crying and cannot talk for few moments. I leave him to peacefully experience all the emotions streaming through his body.

I wondered for a moment how he would treat me but he is looking at me with compassion.

He's telling me it's time to leave this body. He's helping me down and leading me towards the light. I want to apologise to him, but he just presses his finger against my lips, willing me to silence. He needs nothing from me. Instead, he offers me something I'd never known in that life: unconditional love.

At this point, Connor breaks down again. His tears flow freely. Despite the wrongs he had done to this former slave, the man's love is finally releasing him.

The psychic had been right. Connor was carrying the emotional burden of a past life where he was hanged. When he died, the feelings of guilt and worthlessness were not resolved. The energy and nature of those emotions were carried forward into Connor's present life.

We don't know exactly how emotional energy is carried from one life to the next. I suspect such emotions remain timelessly suspended until there is an opportunity for the soul to reconnect with them in a future incarnation. Perhaps we plan a life that will deliberately trigger a reconnection so that the raw, past life emotions surface. This gives us an opportunity for resolution.

It is obvious that these past emotions were present in Connor's current life. And they remained present until he completes the regression. In the session, the slave's love and compassion released his guilt and grief, and gave him a sense of redemption.

Connor later reported that he felt more comfortable wearing a tie. His wife thought he was more at peace within himself and more confident in his business interactions.

Andrew

Andrew came to his regressions with clear expectations. He wanted to know the purpose of his life. He also wanted to remove any blocks that might be preventing him from achieving success with a new business venture.

I begin Andrew's past life session by taking him back to the house where he lived as a child during his current life.

It's a timber house, a Queenslander, and it creaks in the wind like a sailing ship. In summer I sleep beneath a mosquito net. The garden is filled with fruit trees: oranges and mangoes and Queensland nuts. There's a Monstera deliciosa in the shade of the mango tree, and a coffee bush on the other side. Just down the hill there's the orange tree. The oranges are covered in mold.

In front of the house is a liquidambar. It's a magical tree to climb. In spring you're hidden among the green leaves. During winter its leaves turn to gold and spill across the front yard. Then it's like climbing a ship's mast; you can see clear across the roof of the garage and into the neighbour's yard.

These memories help prime Andrew for the next step. I guide him back further, to the age of three months in his current life. He imagines lying in his cot, with his mother looking down at him.

She thinks I'm pretty cute. She's bouncing a red and yellow toy, and I'm laughing at it. She's smiling. She's very happy with me—I'm her firstborn child. I know she loves me.

Next, I take him back to a past life—one which would provide answers to his current dilemmas. He falls silent, as though he is listening intently.

It's night time. There's a deep chill in the air. My name is Henry. I'm wearing a coat, and black leather boots with buckles. The trees in the distance are shaded blue. Everything is silent—dead silent.

The clouds part, and the moonlight shines through. An owl hoots. The moonlight makes me feel anxious. I'm going to meet someone—a rider—who will bring me a message. It's safer not to be seen.

As Andrew relaxes, the information begins to flow freely. Henry is living during the early years of the American War of Independence. He is on the side of the patriots. The redcoats are on the move, and Henry is awaiting news of their intentions. He is thirty years old.

Keeping to the shadows, he rides towards a nearby farm. His neighbour, an older man, ushers him into the kitchen. Henry wants to gain his commitment to the rebels' cause. They converse, but the older man shrugs off Henry's questions. If he chooses the wrong side, he could lose his farm—or worse. Henry leaves, not knowing where his neighbour stands.

He has missed his rendezvous. Has his messenger been captured or killed? Henry heads back to the rebel's camp, taking an indirect route to ensure he is not being followed. He falls in with a rebel scout, and together they return to camp, where they make their report.

Our general is concerned that the British may have captured and interrogated our messenger. Perhaps they have changed their plans as a result. He decides to fall back to the river.

I disagree. If they catch us by the river we will be trapped. The general says he's already planned for this contingency. He has arranged a ferry to carry his troops across the river. But do we have enough time?

I head out again with some other scouts to watch for the enemy. We have two calls: one for all clear, a second one for danger. They sound like birdcalls, so the English will be none the wiser.

I tie my horse to a tree, and climb a low hill. In the distance, a small army is marching our way. There are more of them than we anticipated. With luck, we will have just enough time to cross the river. I place my fingers in my mouth and give the danger call. We all fall back to the ferry.

Meanwhile, another scout has seen a smaller cavalry group advancing from another angle. They'll arrive before we can all escape. Panic ensues. The ferry is overloaded and capsizes midway across the river, sweeping our general to his death. We need to retreat.

The surviving captain takes charge. On the advice of one of the scouts, he sets an ambush. I volunteer to ride out with another man, to lure the redcoats into a narrow valley. They see us, and try to chase us down. We lead them between our hidden comrades, who open fire after we pass. I dismount, and bring an Englishman down with my rifle.

There is no time to reload. My comrade finishes off the Englishman with his sword. As we have the advantage of surprise, our enemy is in disarray. But once they regroup, our lives will be endangered. Our captain knows of a safe place in the mountains where we can hunker down against the coming winter. Maybe the thaw will be kind to us.

Rather than riding together to their hideout, and attracting further attention, the men disperse. Henry heads back for one last look at his farm. As he nears his neighbour's place he hears a commotion. The redcoats have dragged his neighbour from his house, blindfolded him, and placed him against the wall of his barn. A summary execution. Henry knows there is nothing he can do. He has been compromised, and the British will be hunting for him. He will lose his property. He creeps away as a volley of shots rings out.

This experience redoubles Henry's resolve. The only thing that remains to him is his freedom, and he will need to fight to maintain it. He rises up through the ranks of the American army, and becomes an officer. During the next few years he experiences both victory and defeat, but in the end the rebels prevail. Henry wins back his farm, and takes his place in society as a veteran of the War of Independence.

After reflecting on all he has achieved over the years, Henry moves on to the end of his life.

I am lying on my bed, in the same house that I had to abandon so many years ago. There is a candle flickering on the night-stand. I feel the presence of my family surrounding me. I am almost eighty, and have built a prosperous life for myself and my loved ones. My wife, my children and I have lived togeth-er happily, and I know I shall miss them.

Although I am ready to pass peacefully into the next life, there are still several memories that unsettle me.

I am disturbed by the men I saw drowning, while know-ing I could do nothing to help them.

I remember bringing the Englishman down, and my com-rade stabbing him with his sword. It took years of warfare before I became comfortable with killing. If indeed I ever did.

I remember my neighbour trembling against the wall of his barn, waiting for the bullets to rip through his chest. Again, I could do nothing to save him. The range was too great, and even if I killed one or two of the redcoats with my rifle, my neighbour's fate was sealed. And I risked compromis-ing the safety of my comrades, too.

Henry relaxes as his spirit leaves his body, and moves into the light. He senses someone waiting for him, behind the brightness. However, events do not unfold as he expects.

I thought I would be meeting Jesus. Instead, I feel completely at home. It's like the tavern in my hometown. There's a man here who says he's my guide. He asks me how I am feeling.

I tell him that I feel fine. In fact, I feel energised.

He asks me about my life.

I begin my story. As I relate these key events to him, he helps me make sense of them. When my general drowned, I had to act decisively. I survived because I did what was required of me. I had a contribution to make to the war, and my comrades respected me for my knowledge and skills.

My guide has someone he wants me to meet. The Englishman—the one I shot from his horse. To my surprise, he is not angry with me. He says he acted rashly, and paid the price. He has seen his future, and realises that if he had not died he would have risen up to become a strong leader. However, that was not to be.

With the benefit of hindsight, he has come to appreciate the rebels' cause, and sympathises with our situation. Then he says something that astounds me. He says that I have more in common with him that I do with my comrades. We are more imaginative, while they are more practical.

As this thought is sinking in, my guide introduces my old neighbour. He is bitter that the English killed him, because he wasn't ready to die. Even though he had not committed to either side, the redcoats executed him anyway. He knows I could have done nothing to save him. His guides have shown him how his life would have unfolded had he committed to our cause. He would have died later in the war, but with a greater sense of fulfilment. Somehow, this knowledge consoles him.

The soldiers who died in the river? They have moved on to other lives. They came back as another generation of Americans, and helped us realise the fruits of nationhood. I need not mourn for them.

Henry's guide allows him some time to contemplate these encounters in silence. Then, he announces that it is time for him to meet with the Council—not as Henry, but as Andrew. Three other entities come and sit down at the table, and the guide excuses himself.

Again, the three members of the Council present themselves as ordinary people. There is nothing pretentious about them. They speak about Henry's life as a soldier. He learned not just to act, but to also think strategically. That was important. And once the war had been won, he used the same skills to rebuild his life, and to contribute to society.

The Council members agree that it had been a successful life.

Andrew then asks them what lessons he could apply to his current life. The councilors smile, and ask him what he believed the lessons to be. Andrew does not need to think too hard, because the answers immediately begin to flow.

I need to seize opportunities that accord with my conscience, as I did in my life as Henry. I am here to find things that are valuable, and to increase their value by offering them to others. To achieve this, it is important that I be as richly in the moment as often as possible.

I have chosen some challenging responsibilities, both in business and in my personal life. The Council is reminding me that this is a long game. Some issues may take many lifetimes to resolve. Other lives are invested in the same game, and I am here to work with them.

To achieve my purpose, it is clear that I must avoid distractions. Focus on what matters most and move towards my goals.

I must release any blocks that stop me from reaching my goals. While it may not be obvious, I have already been doing this. The most important obstacles to overcome are the inner blocks, because they can paralyse me completely. But I have proven that I can release these blocks. I just need to keep moving forward.

Oh—and there's one last thing. The love I felt from my mother when I was three months old? That's my birthright. We're all entitled to that love. However far we travel, no matter what damage we do to each other, that love is always there, waiting for us to tap into it anew.

Andrew thanks the councilors for their assistance, and returns gradually from his trance. As he reflects on his experience, he realises that redemption requires ongoing forgiveness—of ourselves, and others. He knows that the insights he gained will continue to guide him as he proceeds through his life.

Conclusion

Any guilt we carry yearns to be redeemed, even when it is deeply buried and out of our awareness. When we harbour deep feelings of guilt and unworthiness, our connection with our higher self, as well as our connection with others, is compromised to some degree. We feel empty or unfulfilled. We feel that something is missing from our life.

Love floods into us the moment we feel forgiven. In an instant, we feel cleansed and renewed as this flow of love washes through us. We are changed. We feel lighter and in the coming days and weeks, we start to notice changes. We don't react to some things like we did before. We are more confident in some areas. And some friends or relatives make comments about us being different in some way.

When we embark on our spiritual journey, we do not know exactly what we are going to experience. We trust. We open. We explore. And when we trust and open ourselves up, we sometimes encounter a profound experience of redemption.

Soulmates

*When the one man loves the one woman and the one woman loves
the one man, the very angels desert heaven and come and sit in that
house and sing for joy.*

BRAHMA SUTRA

The idea that we all have been given the challenge of finding our
soulmate has been around a long time. Plato described a soulmate as being one half of a whole. As the story goes, humans
were originally created with both male and female genitalia. This
made them so powerful that they competed with the gods. To reduce their power, the gods split them into two, male and female.
Since then, humans yearn for their other half.

Michael Newton, in his thousands of regressions, investigated the concept of soulmates. Although he accepted that souls do
have a primary soulmate, he found no evidence for the idea of
separated, complementary 'twin' souls.

Being somewhat skeptical, I question the idea that one soul
is bound to another soul indefinitely. My experience this lifetime,
and in the dozens of other lifetimes I have remembered, does not
support this view. I am more inclined to think that we are bound
to another person because of our past.

Perhaps we experienced an unresolved issue with that person
in a previous life. By reincarnating together again, we give ourselves another chance to address this problem. Remember that
this is something we plan before we are born.

Maybe we are missing some quality or characteristic that is

well-developed in our perceived soulmate. We are attracted to the soul that emanates this quality because it makes us feel complete. What we really need to do is develop this quality within ourselves.

Perhaps we have had many incarnations with a particular soul playing the role of our spouse or lover. In subsequent incarnations, we would be naturally attracted to this soul as a romantic partner.

Were several of the above circumstances true of two souls, they would have an extremely powerful attraction to each other.

Some people do have a strong sense that their partner is their soulmate. I have outlined above some reasons why this might be so. However, I do not actually know whether each soul has an eternal soulmate or not.

I do believe, however, that each soul is in the business of developing wholeness or balance. Regardless of gender, we all possess a range of qualities that are usually considered 'masculine' and 'feminine'. For example, a highly assertive woman may be seen by some people to be acting in a 'masculine' fashion, while a highly emotive man may be perceived as 'feminine'. Such cultural stereotypes do not encompass the full range of human behavior, and limit our acceptance of others. Further, if we subscribe to these stereotypes we limit our ability to acknowledge either the 'masculine' or the 'feminine' aspects of our being. In such cases, we can long to meet our soulmate, believing that he or she will compensate for something we have denied within ourselves.

Ultimately, it's our choice whether or not we believe that we have been set the task of finding our soulmate. Here are two cases that might help you decide.

Tahlia

Tahlia comes to a regression because she is struggling in her relationship with her husband. Even though he is having an affair and is very controlling, she believes he is her soulmate. Neither of them is finding it easy to let go, but Tahlia wants to move forward with her life.

She discovers during her session that her husband is her soulmate. Although she loves him and they are strongly connected to each other, she is told she is not meant to continue with him in this life. She needs to develop independence.

> *He is fascinated by the darker world, the Underworld. I am looking over a ledge and I see a dark world. I am not part of it. As husband and wife, I have outgrown him. He just waved at me. We are still connected but I have other things to do.*
>
> *He is confused about breaking up but I see him coping in the long term.*

Tahlia's path is about connecting to her true self, feeling worthy, trusting her intuition and taking action from this understanding. Her guides give her memories from her childhood that reinforce this message.

She goes to a forgotten childhood memory where she meets a lady, a work colleague of her father, who stays with the family for a few weeks.

> *I meet her and jump off a chair, saying, 'Hello, my name is Tahlia and I am six years old.' She is a beautiful, blonde woman, kind, with a lovely energy. My whole being comes*

alive being around her. She sees me and she knows who I am. She knows the beauty in me and there are not many people who recognise that. I can see she is reminding me of who I really am.

Several other memories from childhood also surface. All with the same theme, affirming her as being worthwhile just as she is.

The other person who gives me that same feeling is my Uncle Ken. He loved me just for me, giving me unconditional love. He died when he was only forty and I was about ten.

She is reminded of a photograph she saw of a boy holding a banner over his head. She felt her guides directed her to this golden moment. The banner said, 'I AM GLAD I AM ME!'

This message resonates with her strongly. Later, she sees a playful black panther, waking from a sleep. She identifies with this female panther.

The panther is strong, capable and beautiful and she says, 'Follow me!' We go into an enchanted place, like an old mine shaft lit with candles. Ohh! It opens out and there is a fire in the middle. There are people sitting around the fire. Someone has moved to make room for me and I am saying hello.

Tahlia is given a book in which she can see her future.

There is gold light on the outside of the page and little lights flashing, flowing, fluttering. I see two little pods, like gems. One is a lotus. It opens in my hand and I can feel the warmth. The lotus is a strategy. It is telling me I am ready to take the next step on my path. The other is not yet ready to open.

A year later Tahlia is happy to have left her husband. From his subsequent unreasonable behaviour, she can see more clearly how important it was to be free. As the regression predicted, she is following her path, learning to be self-expressive, true to herself, and intuitive.

Tahlia discovers our soulmate is not always our romantic 'knight in shining armour'. In some lives our soulmate can be difficult. This is part of the plan and designed to help us grow. Tahlia's soulmate, as her husband, was controlling and often dismissive of her. His behaviour helped propel her forward into discovering her self-worth, independent of him.

Rachel

Rachel came to me believing she had met her soulmate. At the same time, she doubted her intuition. Charles works at the station where she catches the train each morning. The moment she first saw him she sensed that she had lost something once and that it was her destiny to recover it. This time, it would be hers to keep. Whenever she noticed Charles on the station platform, she could not help but stare at him—and he could not help but stare back. Although she had never met him before, she felt that she knew him well.

Once, a psychic friend had told Rachel that she would meet her life partner, and that his name would be Charles. This friend was often right, and knowing that gave Rachel the courage she needed. Months before she came for her regression, she gave Charles her phone number. But he never called.

When Rachel reflected on her life, she realised how pervasive was her sense of loss. Even at home there were times when she felt homesick! Was she missing her soulmate? If not, what did that sense of longing mean? Rachel came to her second session with a list of seventeen questions. The most important of these were:

1. Is Charles really my soulmate?
2. When will I meet my soulmate, and what do I need to do to prepare for our meeting?
3. Have I lived a past life with my soulmate?

To begin the session, I ask Rachel if she might find the answers to any of her questions in her current life. She nods, and tells me that the number nine just flashed through her mind. So I take Rachel back to the age of nine.

> It's my cousin's twenty-first birthday party. I'm alone in the TV room with a man I've never met before—one of my cousin's friends. He puts his hands down my pants. I freeze. I don't know how to say 'no'.

We explore her reaction to the assault. Rachel admits that she feels awful. She wishes she had spoken up for herself. As an adult, she realises that this man's behavior was terribly wrong. I encourage her to feel the energy behind the outrage—an energy that wants to say, *how dare you?*

Rachel tunes in to that energy. I take her back to the TV room. Once again, she regresses to the age of nine, but she handles his assault with greater confidence.

> He's sliding his hand towards my crotch. This time, I know that it is wrong, and I speak up for myself. I tell him to stop. He must know that what he's doing is wrong, but he doesn't

stop. He tries to hold me down. This time I'm determined not to freeze.

I tell her to feel her anger. Rachel responds forcefully.

Now I'm kicking and screaming. Mum comes in and pushes him away. She calls out to my uncle—her brother—to kick this guy out. She tells him what he did. My uncle doesn't care. She is annoyed with him and arguing. I am worried Dad will find out. He will be so angry. But the argument between Mum and her brother is getting louder. Dad hears it and comes in. He doesn't like Mum's brothers and how they treat her. He's not sure what's been going on so Mum has to tell him. Dad pushes my uncle aside and tears through the house, looking for this guy. He's holding him up against the wall, hitting and shaking him.

Everyone's trying to pull Dad off this guy, who's now playing the victim. My uncle's yelling at Dad. Dad screams at them to get the fuck out of his house. The party's over. One of my other uncles is telling Dad to relax but Dad turns off the stereo and ushers everyone out. Mum is walking around in a daze, pleading with her guests to leave.

Mum doesn't like or trust men. But if a woman is molested, she blames the woman. She hates herself. When she was my age she was tall, with large breasts. Men noticed. She blamed herself for their sleazy comments, and hated her body. She was afraid of sex, afraid of feeling good. In her mind there was no such thing as date rape. If you show a man any interest, you have to put out. Otherwise, you're nothing but a prick teaser.

She believes it's all up to the woman. Men can't help

themselves. They have absolutely no control over their urges.

After everyone has left the party, Dad is sitting on the bed beside me. I'm too ashamed to speak. Dad tells me that young man had no right to touch me. No one is allowed to do that to a child.

Mum is in the room too. She can't help herself. She still says, 'But what did you do?' She thinks I did something that induced him to touch me.

Dad turns to Mum. 'Don't be ridiculous,' he says. 'She did nothing. She is a little girl. He is not allowed to touch her. No one is allowed to do that.'

It hurts that Mum blames me.

Where did she get that idea that it's my fault?

I assure Rachel that if she really wants to know, she will be given the answer. I can see her struggling with the information she is being offered. It's something she doesn't want to see. She shakes her head. She's pushing back against this idea.

I ask her what messages are coming through.

Rachel cannot speak. I know enough of her family history to guess at the information she is receiving, and it's far from pretty. Rachel's uncles have no respect for her mother, their sister. Rachel's father hates the way those brothers treat his wife. It is a family choked with secrets. Mum's eldest sister was abducted and molested at the age of eight. Rachel's grandfather found the man involved and meted out some vigilante justice. The police were called. No one in the family ever discusses what really happened. None of them believe in dwelling on past wrongs. They just want to get on with it. They're too frightened to look back.

I suggest that the same kinds of strategies may have been played out in previous generations of her family. Rachel frowns.

Mum has always needed to be in control. Blaming women gives her that sense of control. She takes total responsibility for keeping herself safe. Trouble is, she judges others by her standards. But I have nothing to be ashamed of. I'm annoyed that she has projected all of her sins onto me.

I tell Rachel that she is not like the rest of her family. She knows that she has to look at herself and deal with her past if she wants to heal. Rachel manages a wry smile, and tells me that she is the black sheep of her family. Her next story underlines this point.

I have another memory from the age of nine. I was in my room, listening to the radio and dancing around, pretending to be a rock star. Having a blast! Then Mum burst in and told me I should be ashamed of myself, carrying on like that. I'm so embarrassed I hang my head and tell her I'm sorry. Mum is so forceful. She takes up so much space, so much energy. But I did nothing wrong. Even now if I dance and sing around the house I pull myself up. 'Don't be silly!' I tell myself. But it's not my voice. It's Mum's.

Rachel sees that her mother has programmed her to feel ashamed of enjoying herself. This time, however, her mother is not going to win. Rachel allows her mother's criticism to slowly fade away. It's time for Rachel to live her own life, rather than giving so much power to her mother's fears.

Next, I take her back to the age of nine months. This was an awkward time for her and her mother.

Mum is holding me. It's hot and we both feel uncomfortable. Neither of us wants to be there. I think she had me to fill a hole and now she is looking at me and realising that the hole is still empty.

This realisation annoys me. 'I'm not here to fill your hole!' I think. 'I chose the wrong mother.' I want Dad, but my mother won't let me go. Dad is love, pure love. Mum is squeezing me tighter. She wants to stuff me into her hole. She reminds me of Gollum in The Lord of the Rings, *how he coveted The Ring. 'My precious.' But that's not true love. I feel scared. I feel like I am in prison.*

I ask Rachel to imagine the sky opening up for her.

I'm hearing a voice from above. It's not human. It's telling me that when Mum lets me down, look to my father. But he let me down too. He wasn't emotionally available.

He must have shut down to survive. When I was nine months old, he offered me only the purest love. But his love was changed by Mum's darkness.

You might remember that in the chapter, *Emotional Echoes*, Rachel had a past life where she was a cowboy, Joshua, who didn't fully connect with his family. Rachel could not forgive Joshua for shutting down emotionally because he reminded her of her father. In reality, that means she couldn't forgive herself. Her experiences here, with her father, give her a new, comprehensive perspective. She knows how and why one shuts down. With perfect understanding, forgiveness comes automatically.

Mum didn't realise what she had with Dad. It's tragic. She could have healed. He loved her. It was a pure love.

I fear I'm not capable of loving children. I don't want to be like my mother. I want to be able to love children as my father loved me.

I remind Rachel that she is not like her mother and her family, because she is willing to look into the past.

Rachel breathes deeply. She tells me that she feels okay. She is sensing her father's love for her. Having been loved so completely once, she knows she can be loved completely in the future.

Rachel is ready now to move on to a past life. Gently, she allows the cares of her current life to slip away.

I'm on a beach, with a rocky cliff rising behind me. The sea is deep indigo and the sand is pale gold. It feels like California. Big Sur. My name is Miriam.

There's a man with me. He doesn't call me Miriam—he calls me Mary. We've found a little nook at the beach, to shelter us from the wind. We've built a fire. I'm wearing a shirt and shorts over my bikini. It's summer, but there's a chill in the air. We're cooking clams over the fire.

We've been here often, this man and I. His name is Simon and there's a slight chill between us, too. We're not talking. He wants to have children, but I don't. This disagreement has been going on for years. We have a good life together, but my refusal to have children hurts him. Even so, he never throws it back at me. He is a good man. Sensitive. But something in me recoils from the idea of motherhood.

Big Sur is a spiritual place for us. We visited regularly, driving for two hours up the coast. After several decades we moved to live in Big Sur permanently. We bought a house on top of a cliff. Its expansive windows drank in the view of the ocean. I hoped my health would prosper in the Californian climate. But we were not there together long enough.

I'm lying in bed and Simon is holding my hand. I am only sixty, but my heart and lungs have run their race. Simon kisses my hand and I see the tears in his eyes. He tells me that he has no regrets. He loves me. I am beautiful to him. He is going to miss me.

I tell him that I love him too, and that I regret leaving him alone. Now, at the end of my life, I sense the richness that children can bring. Our relationship was strong. Between us we would have created a functional and happy family.

Out of the corner of my eye, I can almost glimpse the children we never had. It is as though they were waiting all along for me to make up my mind, and now it's too late.

I know that Simon will be all right. He will live out his life in this house; he will refuse to die anywhere other than this bed of ours. I pass peacefully, with blackness in my chest. Did Simon offer me something to ease my pain, to ease my death? Maybe.

I'm drifting upwards now. Simon is crying and holding my hand. He knows I'm dead. 'I love you Mary,' he whispers, and I reach down and stroke his hair. He senses my presence, and that comforts him.

From that night on, he slept alone in the middle of our bed. From time to time I visited him, and I was present when he died, many years later. I would stroke his head, and he would feel my warmth around him.

I allow Rachel time to experience and process the emotions that these memories brought to the surface. After a few minutes, she is ready to move on to her life between lives.

I'm in a circular room. It's dark, with gold rectangles on the walls. The windows are mirrors. There's a big wooden table, like you find in libraries. There are no books, but I sense there are books in other rooms. It's quiet. There's a man here. He's going to assess or audit me.

I'm feeling nervous.

He's asking me why I never had kids. I was supposed to have kids.

That was the plan. My life with Simon was set up so we could have children together. It was a safer, kinder, and gentler time than in my current life. If I had children then I would not need to have them now.

I tell him that I just wanted us to be free.

Now he's showing me two little boys. They're impatient to be born. They've been waiting a long time for me to make up my mind, for Charles and I to find each other. It's obvious to me that Simon and Charles share the one soul. The boys even look like Charles. He's the laid-back kind of guy they need as a father.

They're not wild kids but they need us to set gentle boundaries. They need both hugs and freedom. Parents who let them be who they are. Parents who trust them. A mother and father who love each other and trust each other and treat each other with respect. If we can give them all this in their early years, they'll be set for life.

He's just given me their names. The older one is Sami and the younger one is Amos.

But I don't see how it can happen. I'm not financially stable yet. And I'm worried about exposing these kids to my mother. I have to be vigilant about her. I have everything I could want and need. I'm happy and capable, but I've let my mother imprison me.

I have to let go of my fear. I see now that I have some of the same control issues as my mother. But I cannot control everything. I need to be more flexible. My guide is telling me that going on a Vipassana[1] retreat can help me stay calm. He suggests that I do the course I'd been considering in December. That will really benefit me.

Now he's offering me some more advice. He's telling me to lie low at Christmas. Mum wants me to go to the beach with her. He's suggesting I take a swim and find somewhere quiet to read. If it becomes too much I'm to walk away.

He's telling me what to do if I see Charles between now and Christmas. Smile. That's all. Just smile.

After Rachel allows the feelings about her mother to ebb away, she moves on to her next encounter.

My dad is coming to the table. He looks different. His hair is white, and he's lost his goatee. He says he is sorry he isn't stronger. He's tried to protect me as best he could. Mum is his soulmate and he cannot leave her. Her soul is not as old as

---

1 Vipassana is a form of Buddhist meditation that emphasises insight. Retreats are usually silent and can last ten days.

ours. Without him she would tear herself apart. She is very sad. Her life has been hard for a young soul. After they both have died, they'll talk.

He says that I'm strong enough now to fulfil my life's purpose. Being a mother is a necessary step for me. It's something I've avoided in many of my lives…

At this point, Rachel pauses. Something has clearly shaken her.

Dad is asking me something I don't understand. Do I want to meet the Mother Essence?

Sensing her hesitation, I suggest that she accept the invitation. What follows moves Rachel deeply.

She is not my birth mother, but my first mother. My true mother. She is looking at me. Her hands are on my face. She is talking but I cannot hear her.

I tell Rachel that something is getting in the way. When you can see the mouth moving but cannot hear, you are blocking the information for some reason. Soon the reason becomes clear. Rachel is worried that she has let the Mother Essence down. The Mother Essence reassures her before helping her understand her own mother.

She says that there is something I have left undone. I haven't been the teacher to my mother I was meant to be. But I can start now.

I couldn't have done it before. I wasn't strong enough. Even though it will painful, it has to be done. I need to be firm with Mum in a loving way. She'll get upset. I have to allow her to be upset and not hook into it.

I can see Mum shutting down. Curling into herself.

When this happens I have to be careful. Just put an arm around her shoulder for no more than a minute. I have to watch out for her negative energy and get away pretty quickly—that's why I can only hold her briefly. She is very toxic. I am to say nothing—and I'm not to talk to Dad. She thinks that he and I are close, that we exclude her. So I am not to side with Dad. I am to hold her and let her go and Dad will sort out the rest.

I'm being given some clear messages now. I'm never to listen to anything negative Mum says about Charles. If she raises the subject, I'm to stop listening and leave. Later, I'm to tell her why I left.

I'm to let Charles be strong for me.

I'm not to feel guilty if I have a good relationship with Charles and his family, with our children, with my dad.

Remembering that Mum is a young soul will help me be compassionate.

I'm told I'm close to moving up. Advancing as a soul. That's why I felt so isolated during my childhood. I had to do it alone.

Now Simon and Charles are coming to the table. They're one energy, but two men. Their soul energy resonates with mine.

I turn towards Simon first. 'It's good to see you my friend, my forever friend,' he says. 'So good.' We are hugging and laughing. We are joined for one brief eternity.

He takes me back to the beach. I am Miriam but I'm very old, as if I didn't die at sixty. Our grandkids are running around. Those kids are so free. My father is there. The daughter I didn't have is there with her husband. She has a good relationship because of Simon and I. It's like Simon and I are dead, but we've been taken back to watch our family at play.

He says, 'I know it doesn't feel like it, but you can have this in your current life. I know you are scared. There will be so much love between us all, you won't notice.'

I've come back to the table in the circular room now. He kisses me on the head—he's gone.

Charles is here now. He says he is going to take care of me and love me. He says that I'm not like my mother. Sami and Amos are waiting for me, so hurry up. He is waiting too.

It still doesn't feel real.

I need to believe in myself and in him.

He tells me why he never rang after I gave him my phone number. 'You weren't ready. You were carrying too much negativity from your mother, and hurt from your father. I knew you didn't want children.' He has something important to tell me. 'We won't be together unless you desire to have children with all your heart. And you have to desire those children for your sake—not for theirs, not for mine. When you are ready, I will know.'

I say, 'I am ready now.'

Mum has programmed me to believe that I'm not worthy. But she's not going to stand between me and my destiny.

There is nothing Charles can do if I don't believe in myself. But any time that negative programming kicks in, I will just have to work through the discomfort, keep breathing deeply and remember who I am. Charles and I are going to help each other heal.

He is ready for those boys. I get a strong sense of love and satisfaction seeing the three of them together.

It feels real now.

The three of them—Charles and Sami and Amos—are waiting for me on the beach. I'm going to them. They are so happy to see me. I say, 'I'm sorry I took so long.' They don't care. We're together now.

Charles tells me that if ever our relationship feels uncomfortable, I'm to remember that it's meant to be. We have done it before.

Rachel emerged from her session with a serenity she had never experienced before. She knew that Charles was her soulmate; that they had shared a loving life together in the past and they would so again in the future.

After Rachel's session, I continued to wonder if Charles was her soulmate and if she was destined to be with him this life. She had given him her phone number over a year before her first session and it was his failure to call that brought her to her first regression.

About a year after our original sessions, Rachel came back for a further regression. She had continued her healing journey, reading books, doing yoga and meditation. She had seen Charles nearly every day, but she had never spoken to him again. Instead she discovered, by a strange coincidence, that he was already married. With this discovery, she recalled a dream she had not long after she'd given him her phone number.

In the dream Charles was standing with a woman who he had just proposed to. He turned to me and said, 'I am sorry. You are just too late.'

Rachel was so upset by the dream at the time, she'd put it out of her mind. But right now she wasn't upset at all. She still didn't want children and she was more relieved than disturbed that she was not going to create a family with Charles this life.

During her second life between lives regression, we took the opportunity to ask her guide, Malachi, about this turn of events.

Malachi said my heart is still stone and that can be no more. This is a turning point lifetime for me. That is why I saw myself with Charles and our potential children on the beach. That isn't one of the paths for this life, but I came into contact with him and his energy to start opening my heart. It had to be more than a dream. It needed to feel real. This was the safest way to do it. I could open up without fear.

Over the past few months, I realised that everything I needed to be, in order to be with him and make it work, wasn't yet there. That is why I felt relief when I found out he was married. But the door has opened now, and I can feel my stony heart, whereas before I couldn't.

I could have damaged my soul if I had another lifetime with Charles while having a closed heart. That is why I am so tired, weighed down with a heart heavy from carrying the pain of the past.

He is a soulmate, Malachi is telling me. We have had a lot of lifetimes together. I only saw him from the outside. He is not smart this lifetime and not confident in himself. He got a great confidence boost when I gave him my phone number. His mates know about it and he needed that.

What I am experiencing is a carefully designed process. I wasn't ready for the truth in the last regression. Giving people more than they are ready for is damaging.

While I was on my own, waiting for him, I was clearing out so much emotional baggage. I did the Vipassana, energy healing, journaling and meditating. I also realised I am okay being alone. Having people around is a bonus rather than a necessity. I kept myself on hold for him for eighteen months, growing emotionally. And more growing is coming. It is about trust, going with the flow, knowing I am safe and not having to be in control.

Rachel came to many more regressions. We still wanted to know why she didn't want children and why she had a stony heart. We discovered the answers, which I will share in my next book.

Rachel was also told that she has another soulmate waiting for her. She incarnates frequently with him as a partner, but the tone of those lives is different to the lives she has with Charles. Charles's soul likes to grow slowly in easier lives while this new soulmate has been willing to take on more challenging lives. Malachi gives her some advice.

There is a very strong man not far away. He is similar to you, and although he is older, he is young at heart. He is soft. Be careful with his heart. You will need to be the kindest person you can be, and at all times. Listen to guidance and don't go into the ego and react. Be honest and express your true feelings with him. When you love, you can feel comfortable even while feeling vulnerable. Accept yourself Rachel, you are lovely. Don't be negative about yourself to you or to him. Be kind and gentle with him. Be kind and gentle with yourself.

Three years later Rachel is with her new soulmate. Matthew is sixteen years older than she is, a lovely gentleman who I was privileged to meet. Malachi was right. He said this man was not far away and he had also told her to keep up her regular run at the park. Matthew actually lived nearby, and she saw him on her runs. Eventually they met.

Rachel took Malachi's advice and she and Matthew are having a wonderful time together.

Conclusion

Clearly, Tahlia and Rachel both believe in the concept of soulmates. The evidence they received during their sessions supported this belief. It also helped them to make sense of their life experiences, and the attraction they felt towards their respective soulmates. As a result, they felt at peace and went on with their lives with a renewed sense of purpose.

If the idea of having a soulmate is correct, Tahlia's case demonstrates that you are not necessarily meant to be *with* that person all through your life. Michael Newton had many cases that confirmed this principle.

From the many regressions I have conducted, I have concluded that spending your life hoping your soulmate will appear is not a good idea. One case in particular illustrates the folly of obsessive romanticism.

In a past life, Phillip was a castle guard. Phillip spent his whole life desiring the lord's daughter. The Council of Elders pointed out the futility of this behaviour. He could have married and had a happy, satisfying life. He was told that some of the things we desire are not within our reach. His obsession with the lord's daughter was designed to teach him a valuable lesson—but only after he realised the pointlessness of his desire. He could not find happiness until he let go of his infatuation with an unattainable woman.

Our lives are fluid. Many forces and influences come together to make a life. Our existence as a soul is dynamic. We have countless lifetimes playing many different roles, having many different experiences and creating many different relationships. I am sure we create numerous diverse alliances with numerous diverse souls. Whether or not one relationship is exclusively the strongest is a mystery—a mystery that each of us must solve to our own satisfaction.

Conclusion

Gratitude is not only the greatest of virtues, but the parent of all others.

CICERO

In this book I have canvassed the regressions of over fifty people. In telling their stories, I wished to give you a taste of what it is like to visit your past life or your life between lives. I have explored the reasons why people undertake regressions and I have demonstrated some of the benefits. There are good reasons for the choice of cases. Some were representative of the types of questions that people bring to regressions. Some were interesting in their own right. Some were illuminating and informative. Some were detailed and picturesque. Some explored the greater questions of life.

A past life regression takes up to three hours. A visit to your life between lives can be as long as five hours. This is a substantial investment of time and money. So far, everyone I have regressed has been pleased with his or her investment.

I give my clients a recording of the session for further contemplation. The recording does not always include the hypnotic induction. Nevertheless, listening to the recording will usually take them back into their life between lives. By listening to their recording several times, they can build a neural pathway in their brain, which will help them connect to their guides. Eventually they can connect without the recording. This gives them the opportunity to receive valuable information and continual guidance.

I would never persuade anyone to do a regression, especially those who are reluctant. The people who come to undertake these journeys are guided to do so.

You will know if such a journey is right for you. If you are not sure, the idea of undertaking a regression will keep recurring. Eventually you will know if it is the next step to take. If so, you will feel compelled to make this particular investment in your spiritual journey.

There are over two hundred people like myself scattered around the world. They are certified as life between lives hypnotherapists by The Newton Institute and listed on the Institute's website.[1] While we have different personalities and backgrounds, we all follow the approach given to us through the pioneering work of Michael Newton.

While I provide in-person consultations in the hinterland of the Sunshine Coast, I also conduct regressions over the Internet, working with clients from all around the world. These sessions have all been successful, and some clients prefer this approach. They appreciate the convenience and the sense of safety that undergoing a regression in the familiar surroundings of their own home confers.

From time to time, my TNI colleagues and I regress each other. We contact our guides and ask for advice. Several times, our guides have counselled us to spread the word about the healing power of knowing about our past lives and our life between lives. That is the reason I have written this book.

---

1 Website: newtoninstitute.org

If you have enjoyed the stories in this book, and found them informative or helpful, I would greatly appreciate your help in spreading the word. You could do this by telling others who might be interested, blogging about it, posting references to this book on social media, subscribing to my blog,[2] Twitter[3] or Instagram[4] feeds, or by writing reviews on Amazon and other relevant websites.

Some of the case studies presented here may have raised questions in your mind. If so, you're welcome to contact me through the website. Your questions will help shape the intentions for my later books, which will use compelling information from many regressions to shed light on our current lives. I am particularly interested in the reasons we fall into darkness and how we emerge into light, which is the journey many of our souls take from our first incarnation to our last.

The most exciting part of conducting these regressions is the change I see in my clients. When we visit these realms in our life between lives, we are loved unconditionally. As a result, we return with renewed vigor and appreciation for our physical life. We learn to value the challenges that we face as we undertake our human journey.

I remember when I was just eight years old, I wrote a school essay about heaven. It was fairly clichéd—the streets were paved with gold and everything one could ever desire was available. The teacher read it out to the class. After complimenting me on my effort, he said I had missed something. 'What,' he asked, 'is the

---

2 Website: lifebetweenlivesregression.com.au
3 Twitter: @KarenJoyAuthor
4 Instagram: KarenJoyAuthor

problem with living in a place like heaven where all is perfect and you receive everything you want?'

I found his question confusing. Heaven sounded wonderful to me. 'What could possibly be wrong with perfection?' I thought. I never forgot his answer. 'You would soon be totally bored. You would have nothing to do and nothing to strive for.' I thought about it and soon realised he was right.

We might curse our challenges and bemoan the effort we need to exert to overcome them. But they are truly a blessing. The joy of success only comes to those who have felt the pain of struggle. Our life is a gift. When we reconnect with the realm of our life between lives, our dedicated guides and our wise elders remind us of the value of this great gift.

Further Reading

The Newton Institute *Llewellyn's Little Book of Life Between Lives* Llewellyn, 2018
This book is a useful introduction to the hypnotic process utilised to access past lives and our life between lives. I wrote this book in conjunction with three other members of the Newton Institute's Research Committee. We illustrate our points with cases drawn from our clients' personal journeys.

Michael Newton *Journey of Souls* Llewellyn, 2003
Destiny of Souls Llewellyn, 2001
These books are invaluable for anyone interested in life between lives regression. Michael pioneered these spiritual journeys. In these books, he summarises and outlines the experiences of his many clients.

Robert Monroe *Journeys out of the Body* Broadway, 1992
Far Journeys Broadway, 1992
Ultimate Journey Broadway, 1996
After Robert Monroe spontaneously went out of body, he started researching this phenomenon. His three books record his journey over thirty years, culminating in the establishment of the Monroe Institute.

Thomas Campbell *My Big TOE* Lightning Strike Books, 2007
Thomas Campbell is a physicist who has worked for NASA. His comprehensive theory of the nature of reality fills over 800 pages. Alternatively, Campbell's two-hour talk to the Monroe Institute is available on YouTube. It provides a clear introduction to his ideas. He suggests that we live in a virtual reality and our

universe has an inherent drive to lower entropy. Reincarnation is a part of this process.

Brian Weiss *Many Lives, Many Masters* Touchstone, 1998
Brian Weiss stumbled across past lives as a psychiatrist. He wrote this best-selling book about his experiences of past life regression and the journey of one of his clients.

Ian Stevenson, M.D. *Reincarnation and Biology: A Contribution to the Etiology of Birthmarks and Birth Defects* Praeger Publishers, 1997
Over a career spanning forty years, Dr. Ian Stevenson investigated three thousand young children who claimed they remembered past lives. Two hundred of the most persuasive cases are presented in this huge masterwork. Volume One deals with birthmarks, while Volume Two deals with birth defects. Dr. Stevenson's writing is academic in style and is only recommended for the serious researcher.

Tom Schroder *Old Souls: Compelling Evidence From Children Who Remember Past Lives* Fireside, 2001
Washington Post journalist, Tom Schroder, accompanied Professor Ian Stevenson on one of his field trips and reports his observations. Dr Stevenson, a psychiatrist, spent forty years researching children who appeared to have lived past lives. Tom, a sceptic when he started this investigation, was forced to open his mind to the possibility of past lives as the evidence mounted.

Eben Alexander *Proof of Heaven, a Neurosurgeon's Journey into the Afterlife* Simon & Schuster, 2012
Eben Alexander died and went to heaven. This well-written book

strongly refutes the theory that the brain remains operational during a near-death experience.

Cherie Sutherland *Children of the Light: Near Death Experiences of Children* Souvenir Press, 1996
Cherie Sutherland records the stories of eighteen children who provide, in their own words, compelling evidence of life after death.

Ann J. Clark, Karen Joy, Joanne Selinske, Marilyn Hargreaves *Wisdom of Souls*, Llewellyn, published December, 2019.
This book draws upon over sixty cases, contributed by twenty-five Newton Institute Practitioners from around the world, to help us navigate some of life's greatest challenges. These stories show us how to shift our perspective from confusion and despair to joy and understanding.

Acknowledgements

I am extremely grateful to all my clients and particularly to those whose stories are told in this book.

Once I had completed my draft manuscript, I asked a number of people to read it and provide me with feedback. To Terry Domico, Belinda Hodge, Jane Teresa Anderson, Candice Lambert and Erica Duguid, I offer my heartfelt thanks. Your comments and encouragement have been invaluable. The book has been made stronger due to your generosity and consideration.

My greatest debt is to my husband, Ian Demack. It is impossible to express in words the gratitude I feel. As well as being a loyal and supportive husband, he has mentored me as a writer for two decades. My writing skills have improved immeasurably as a consequence. As well he has patiently coached me and supported me during the writing of this book. As a professional editor and published author, he has done a superb job of editing this book. He ensured that the book is well-expressed and easy to read while remaining true to the intentions behind the book and the stories within it.

About the Author

Karen Joy lives in the hinterland of Queensland's Sunshine Coast, Australia, where she writes and works as a spiritual counsellor, conducting present life, past life and life between lives regressions, in-person and over the Internet.

To learn more, visit: lifebetweenlivesregression.com.au.

Please feel welcome to log on and subscribe to Karen's monthly blog.

Before qualifying as a life between lives practitioner, Karen spent twenty years as the principal of a counselling practice, seeing clients as a psychologist. For a decade, she wrote a popular column on emotional issues in *The Courier Mail*, Brisbane's daily newspaper. Karen drew on these writings to compile her *Relationship Mysteries Revealed* series, which is available on Kindle through Amazon. *Other Lives, Other Realms* is her first book on spiritual matters. Since 2014, Karen has been a member of The Newton Institute Research Committee. The four members of this committee continue the work of Michael Newton, doing research into Life Between Lives and writing books for Michael's publisher Llewellyn. The first of these books, *Llewellyn's Little*

Book of Life Between Lives, was published in October 2018, and the second, *Wisdom of Souls,* is scheduled for publication in late 2019.

Karen lives with her husband Ian Demack, and their poodle cross, Harry. Niccolò, the elegant cat appearing with Karen in the photograph above, passed away before this edition came into print. Karen enjoys travel, music, movies, ballet, opera and art. She has two children, five grandchildren and two great grand-children.

If you enjoyed *Other Lives, Other Realms...*

'Someone is going to die. There must always be a sacrifice.'

Alone in the rainforest, haunted by the ghosts of failures past, acclaimed landscape photographer Daniel Lucinge faces a stark choice: to confront the demons lodged within his psyche, or remain forever lost.

Beyond Majestic carries you deep into the vast nocturnal world of the imagination. By turns provocative, insightful and lyrical, it charts Daniel's journey to reclaim his essential majesty—and recapture his creative mojo.

This beautifully written book reveals a compelling truth—that each one of us is the hero of his or her own spiritual journey.

KAREN JOY

Beyond Majestic will be published by MediaLuna in 2019
Paperback edition: 978-0-9942567-4-4
eBook edition: 978-0-9942567-6-8

Made in the USA
Middletown, DE
04 May 2021